About the Author

Jamie Davies was born and raised in Cardiff where she lives with her gorgeous husband, beautiful but very sassy daughter, crazy puppy and two very arrogant cats. When Jamie is not multitasking and playing servant to her ever demanding threenager, she loves to: holiday, drink cocktails, eat delicious food, party in the kitchen and spend time with her family. In her late twenties, Jamie stumbled onto the conclusion that the grey suit and briefcase bullshit of a corporate career probably wasn't for her. Inspired by the mind-fucking experience of motherhood Jamie turned her focus to writing her first book, *Motherfuckinghood*.

Motherfuckinghood

Jamie Davies

Motherfuckinghood

Olympia Publishers
London

www.olympiapublishers.com
OLYMPIA PAPERBACK EDITION

Copyright © Jamie Davies 2023

The right of Jamie Davies to be identified as author of
this work has been asserted in accordance with sections 77 and 78 of
the Copyright, Designs and Patents Act 1988.

All Rights Reserved

No reproduction, copy or transmission of this publication
may be made without written permission.
No paragraph of this publication may be reproduced,
copied or transmitted save with the written permission of the publisher,
or in accordance with the provisions
of the Copyright Act 1956 (as amended).

Any person who commits any unauthorised act in relation to
this publication may be liable to criminal
prosecution and civil claims for damage.

A CIP catalogue record for this title is
available from the British Library.

ISBN: 978-1-80074-902-3

This is a work of creative nonfiction. The events are portrayed to the
best of the author's memory. While all the stories in this book are true,
some names and identifying details have been changed to protect the
privacy of the people involved.

First Published in 2023

Olympia Publishers
Tallis House
2 Tallis Street
London
EC4Y 0AB

Printed in Great Britain

Dedication

I dedicate this book to my beautiful daughter, without whom this book wouldn't exist. My love for you is ever growing and never ending. My journey with you is one I will treasure forever. I love you always x

Acknowledgements

Thank you to my ever-loving husband for your support, encouragement and never-ending belief in me. I love you x

The Intro to the Intro

I felt I needed to add this before the nitty gritty shit storm of my newborn phase begins. Just in case you are in the nitty gritty shit storm phase right now, then perhaps you need a bit of a softer start than the actual start!

I wrote this book every day (pretty much) along my journey of motherhood. And now as I finish this, I have made this addition – so I start here and not at the 'original intro'. To let you know that as you read my darkest, bleakest moments that I share – right now as my daughter is two and a half years old, I wish for more. I wish to do it all again. Given the option I would have another ten children, though I would settle for just one more. For a number of reasons, selfish ones; to feel that tiny human growing inside me, to watch my belly grow, to carry a miracle inside my body, to meet that new person that was a part of my body for nine months and to see the little person they become. What makes them laugh, cry, what they like, don't like – to watch that little, teeny tiny human grow into their own little tiny person. To watch them take their place in our little family and to discover what quirks they bring (to an already quirky bunch), but most of all to give my perfect tiny human a sibling, a playmate, a forever friend. Someone who always got their back – even if sometimes they really annoy each other!

I thought this was important to add here because as you read my story, my feelings, my experiences especially in the earliest days if you are at the start of your own story right now and my experiences are hitting home, I don't want you to be afraid. To fear that the long, dark lonely days are how it is going to be. They are so short lived. These days will pass quickly. Soon your tiny human will become a little person, your best friend, the person you do everything for. The person you put before your every single need. Tough days are always there – but that's life. A bad day, sometimes a bad week but fulfilled in its entirety by so many happy, magical, fun moments – completely and totally overwhelming love.

They say that mothers who birth another child must forget the pain of childbirth, the exhaustion of those early years, the putting oneself at the bottom of the pile to meet every need of your child – I disagree. I think we just know that to do it all again is worth it all.

Those short-lived painful, emotional, exhausting days, weeks and months are worth it for a lifetime fulfilled with the love and enjoyment that are to come.

Enjoy these moments – that used to piss me off when people would say that. But honestly, I miss every single moment of those first weeks and months. The hardest days especially because what I thought was damaging both me and my tiny human was actually just the beginning of us. It was shaping us, we were teaching each other, we were learning how to be with one another, how to cope in despair, when the whole world around us was carrying on and we felt trapped physically and mentally we were learning to just be.

So, know that for every dark moment that you will undoubtedly live and feel in the next few weeks and months you will be rewarded with a thousand times those moments in love, laughter and enjoyment.

The 'Original' Intro – Let's Be Real

Cesarean - definition of cesarean by The Free Dictionary –
1. (sometimes cap.) Also called ***cesar'ean*** *sec`tion. an operation by which a fetus is taken from the uterus by cutting through the walls of the abdomen and uterus.*

A pain so intense. So raw. So indescribable. So real yet so unimaginable! The unbearable pain of childbirth – I had a caesarean.

In the moment of such intense pain, your stomach having been ripped open, a tiny human physically pulled out of you – you, this same you who is still being sewn back together is then handed the tiniest, precious human whose life is quite literally in your hands!

Is there any other surgery like this? Any other surgery where you are awake, opened up, stitched back together and then handed a new life to look after. After this surgery there is no recovery, there is no lovely little guardian angel who pops by and says, "Here you go, my dear, have a nice rest now, heal, come around from this major surgery you have just gone through and I will take care of things until you are back on your feet." No, no, no – it is time to shape up and literally start as you mean to go on – second place. It is your time to shine at being that parent you have imagined yourself to be. The imagining you have spent the last nine months doing with all kinds of unrealistic expectation. No time to rest and recover, no time to rest that wound – you need to get up, get a grip and care for this tiny, gorgeous baby.

I don't even think I can get close to the level of pain with words, but I will try my best. For clarity the pain comes after the surgery, you are so drugged up for the actual procedure that the sensation is all you feel, but the pain that follows – wow!

Imagine for a second that you have just been run over by a lorry, that same lorry has not only run over you but has then reversed back over your battered, aching body and for good measure run over you again. Just when you are thinking what the fuck is happening to my body you are handed a tiny human whose life you are completely responsible for. This tiny human will scream ALL of the time, there is nothing terribly wrong with tiny human; they are hungry, want a cuddle and possibly have wind. You will be scared of tiny human, your own shadow and all other humans for a little while but rest assured this unimaginable fear will only last this intensely for a few weeks. By this point you will be so tired that you will start to give less of a shit and that fear will ease. Until that point dig deep, drain every bit of support you have around you and know that mama you're doing a great job. This tiny human just needs to feel loved, secure, be fed and bathed and before you know it you will start to feel like you're doing a good job (most of the time anyway)!

I sent these words to my wonderful cousin in her first week of motherhood. A message I wish that I had received in my first week as a mama to know that what I was going through was normal! That what I was feeling was normal! That motherhood is actually that hard, that tough and that fear, that overwhelming fear is normal!

In my first weeks as a mama I was sure that I was spiraling into the deepest depths of postnatal depression. As I write this now, I am not convinced that I wasn't. I have read a lot about postnatal depression since, and it is possible, likely in fact, that I was suffering. All I do know is that whatever it was left me as quickly as it came – kind of! The fear began to ease when she was fourteen weeks old and eventually by week sixteen (yes, I can be that specific) it became enjoyable. I am no pink fluffy mummy by the way – not every day is enjoyable, some days are really shit! The days when you are hormonal will often be the same days that your tiny human is being completely irrational from the moment they open their eyes. Those days will always be the days that you watch the clock so intently that you see every hour that passes by. You look forward to bedtime, their bed time so that you can sit by yourself and enjoy the quiet, enjoy wallowing in your hormonal state watching the shittiest, girly Netflix box set that you can find – but they are different kind of problems! 'Normal' life problems!

The sole purpose of antenatal classes in my opinion should be to really prepare us for those first days, weeks and months of parenthood. To be frank my antenatal class was a pile of shit. I went to one; the topic covered – labour. The purpose of this class was to teach us expectant parents how to recognise labour, explain the different stages of labour and to educate us on what is happening during the birth. There was a second class that the midwife referred to as the 'scary' one, she told us nervous, naive and excited expectant first-time parents that we didn't need to attend the second class. It covered 'when things go wrong'. Being a gullible first timer, of course there was to be no complications during my labour. Why would there be! If only I knew then what my labour would entail, I would have been there, front row with my notebook. The truth is, in my opinion, you can't prepare for labour, not really. If you are a first-time mama then you have no idea how your body is going to respond to labour, you definitely have no idea how your baby is going to respond to labour and despite what you are told in those many antenatal appointments you attend neither do the best doctors and midwives around.

Antenatal classes should teach us the practical things that we so desperately need to know in those first days, weeks and months. I'm talking the real basics; how to make bottles, how to sterilise, what to do if your baby wont feed, wet nappies, dirty nappies, bathing, new baby rash, how long to feed on demand, when to be worried, when to seek help and support. The things that you spend all of those early days doing and the things that send you into total despair for most of those days. More importantly than this, they should prepare you for the emotional strain, the mental strain, the exhaustion. They should educate us on how you should expect to feel, how long those feelings should last, when to suspect that you may have postnatal depression and how to seek support. Those to me are the most important things and the only things you can give to a new mama to give her some kind of realistic expectation. This information would enable her to prepare somewhat for what is about to happen mentally and emotionally when this tiny human arrives.

Though after having been through it, I do honestly believe there is no way you can prepare for it, not completely. The expectation versus the reality is too wide a gap, it's colossal.

Your life as you knew it has gone. I mean completely disappeared. You are still you but the person you were is watching you from across the room through squinted eyes and you are looking back at her, reaching for her, grieving her.

When you talk to those 'already parents' nobody tells you the truth, the whole truth. Nobody talks about the fear, the loneliness, the anxiety, the exhaustion, the pain, the tears, the sweating, the paranoia, the, 'Please God will someone take this tiny human away and give me back my old life.' To talk about this is to accept that there were so many moments you regretted bringing this perfect, innocent, beautiful tiny human into this world. You are admitting that there were times that you really did not want this. You did not want to be a mama. You did not want to be a parent. You were so convinced that this was exactly what you needed to fulfil you, but you had been so wrong in your thinking. Awful I know that's what you may be thinking but in those dark lonely nights that's what you think. When you feel you really cannot do this you wish that someone could make it all go away.

Why would anyone talk about this? Why would you openly talk about the shameful truth when the whole time you know you should be grateful, you know you should be enjoying every moment. You have waited and longed and prayed to the greatest powers for your bundle of joy. You may or may not have been through your own epic journey to create this beautiful, perfect tiny human. Whatever your story is, for those first six weeks (and some) all you can think about is when this living nightmare will be over.

I know that not every single mother feels this way, for those lucky enough they will find it a breeze. They are natural born mothers – they do exist, I have met them, I envied them once but not now. They have no fear. They really do enjoy those first days, weeks and months. Even after all this I wouldn't want to change my story, it was hard, but it was mine and looking back it was perfect!

What I do know is this, when I have borne my soul to many of my new mama friends and those who have been parents for many years they have not gasped in horror at my awful truths. They have barely flinched. What they have done is smiled and nodded, shared their deepest darkest truths too – so it seems that most of us go through these weeks and months, but no one says a thing about it because to the outside world, to those around us – these should be the best days of our lives.

This perception is damaging – from the moment you become pregnant everything is new and exciting and all that is talked about is this wonderful human you are creating, the new bottle machines, these fabulous baby monitors, the oh-so-cute baby clothes. On this platform why would anyone feel okay about sharing their shit show of their first few weeks as a mama, to go against the perception of the entire freaking world because of course they should be so happy and walking on cloud nine in crazy love with their newborn right? I mean to say that you don't feel an overwhelming love, to say you feel scared, annoyed, filled with nothing but anxiety which leaves you no room for overwhelming love whatsoever. The truth is that it is hard, really bloody hard! For some reason this seems to be a taboo subject – something to hide from those closest to you, something to deny to yourself, something to try and pretend is not real.

Is it the pressure of society? There is definitely a self-pressure – why? I found myself constantly making comparisons to those mamas around me who seemed to 'have this'. It wasn't just me making these comparisons; family members were doing this too. They would often tell me just how well so and so down the road was doing, she is going to this class and that class, she is never in the house, blah blah fucking blah! I don't know where the pressure comes from, but for those struggling there is a pressure that we should 'have' this, we should be able to 'cope' with this and worse still that we should be good at this.

In your reality you find yourself sweating your way through your first days and weeks of being a mama with not a fucking clue of what you are doing or even what you are supposed to be doing. You feel like shit, the lowest you have ever felt, you look like shit, every inch of your body aches. Your stomach yearns for nourishment because it is five p.m. and you haven't even thought about putting a piece of food in your mouth because really there is no time.

You finally have a wee and it hurts and stinks because you have been holding it in for the last nine hours because you really didn't have time. Then you hear the dreaded words that you have been waiting to hear, the, 'I don't understand this; you've wanted this baby for so long. All you have ever wanted is this baby and now you've got what you've always wanted you feel like this.' These words don't shock you because since this tiny human has arrived you have said these words to yourself every single day. You have also tried your best to hide your feelings because you know this is what those around you will think. However, that does not take the sting out of those words. It is like a kick in the face, an expectant one but nevertheless a bloody painful kick. You have not the energy to react. You just add it to your list of things to feel shit about. I must point out here that my husband is a wonderful person, and I am confident that as he uttered those words he did not know just how broken I was or how much I was struggling (because I did try my best to hide it from him). Those words were spoken many times in that first year when we would reminisce so all I can assume is that it is a factor only understandable if you just accept that men are from Venus and women are from Mars. A concept that, I not only didn't understand but that I completely disagreed with before having a baby.

You are fighting your own battle; you don't want to accept you are struggling but know that you are. You don't even allow your brain to consider that you could be suffering with postnatal depression, you can't allow it because the reality is that it is very likely. You want to be enjoying every moment because you worry that when this time has passed you will regret not embracing these days. This daily battle is tough. For me, avoidance was key in those early days. I did not post my news on social media – I was living a nightmare and I did not want the outside world to find any joy in my tiny human when I could not. I didn't open the many cards and gifts of congratulations we had received because this was something to enjoy and of all the feelings I had, enjoyment was definitely not one of them!

Visitors were another dread. I'm not talking distant friends here; I am talking closest family members. The thought of her being passed around would definitely cause her distress and worse than that was the thought of trying to console an inconsolable baby with an audience, this made me severely nauseas. The worst part of all of this is EVERYONE wants to come and meet your tiny human. EVERYONE is excited to meet your tiny human, and EVERYONE wants to cuddle your tiny human. This leaves you with a feeling of nothing but dread, fear and anxiety!

The truth is that you are petrified, your whole being is overwhelmed with fear. All of the wonderful feelings you should be feeling are entirely overshadowed by this awful fear. When those around you tell you how beautiful your tiny human is, how you must be so proud, how you must be besotted you just smile and nod. In truth these 'statements', these assumptions piss you off because you don't feel any of those things and worse than that, you know that you probably should. This tiny human is ruining my life so no, I am not proud and I am definitely not besotted. Why can't you understand this? Why can't you ask how

I am feeling instead of assuming?! And if someone dares to tell you that you have such a good baby, punch them in the face. When you have been up all night with a screaming, inconsolable tiny human whilst that smug shit of a visitor has enjoyed a peaceful night's sleep how dare they have the audacity to tell you what a good baby you have! Try this for a week my friend and then, and only then can you tell me what a good baby I have!

Looking back this tiny human was not ruining my life; she was definitely ruining my sleep but not my life. It's a whirlwind, this tiny bundle who causes almighty chaos arrives, your calm, peaceful, organised life goes completely to shit but then somewhere along the way the whirlwind stops. Some sort of calm returns and you start to rebuild your life – a different kind of life to the one that was there before the whirlwind erupted. You are stronger having weathered the storm but still somewhat lost from the life that was there before.

Why am I writing this? Why would I bare my awful truths to an audience of complete strangers? Because I wish I had been given the whole truths, I wish I had been prepared for the highs and lows of the first days and weeks of welcoming my beautiful daughter into the world. Maybe it would have eased my anxieties and fears. Made me enjoy and appreciate those first days more, instead of wishing the days away in the hope, that if they quickly passed she would get older and this would be over, things would be easier. I wouldn't be petrified and I would find the person I once was. The person who was completely lost from the moment that wonderful, innocent, perfect baby was placed in her arms. I could see her, the person I once was but she was in a daze, the hellish days were merging, and the living nightmare had robbed her of any happiness, enjoyment, conversation, interest, and appetite. I was lost, so very lost and frightened that I would never find myself, worse still that I would never 'have' this.

Six weeks I kept reading about this bloody six weeks, people kept saying just get through the first six weeks and you will feel like super woman. The thought of six weeks of living this hell everyday was unbearable; I wasn't convinced I could get through the next six hours so there was no chance I could get through the next six weeks. But I did and you will too because you are amazing, you have a strength within that you do not know exists until you get through this, so hang on in there!

I promise not to make this a depressing read, I want to share this with you to tell you that these days pass quickly. Soon your beautiful baby will provide you with nothing but pure joy and amazement of the best kind every single day. You will miss them when they sleep and look forward to that early morning wakeup call just so you can spend every single waking moment watching their precious little face; smile at you when you peer into their cot, explore things for the first time, laugh at you, look at you for reassurance when they see a new face, hold you so tightly when they are upset. All of these precious moments of pure enjoyment and love are only weeks away.

I hope to give you a few laughs to help you through your lonely days and know that even in your loneliest most vulnerable state there is another mother somewhere else feeling exactly the same as you do. So don't panic, hold tight, scream if you want to go faster and enjoy the ride because those first few weeks pass by so quickly and I promise you when they are over, guess what – you will wish to relive them all over again!

I am going to share with you all of my pivotal moments as a first-time mama; the good, the bad and the ugly! Not exclusively the first six weeks because for me although the screaming eased, I was still not my whole self, I was still overshadowed by that overwhelming fear until she was fourteen weeks old. Even after that we had a few 'experiences' but they were far outweighed by the highs. So, whether you're pregnant or just entering your first days as a mama and thinking what the fuck has happened to my life I hope that you can read this and rest assured that you are normal and the end of this looming darkness is right around the corner!

We survived our first year and this is how it went…

Our Story, The Short Version!

Everyone tells you 'not to think about it' when trying for a baby and it will happen. These are the same people who never had to think about it.

We tried for our precious baby girl for three years. Years of tears, longing, desperation and pure emptiness trying so desperately to fill that gaping hole in my heart of where that baby should be. I knew I would never be complete without a baby and whatever it took or however long it took I had to have a baby. My life would always be incomplete and so unfulfilled without one. We had a good life, a great life. We were and are strong as a couple, we had great times and we had made so many wonderful memories, however, I knew that for me it wasn't enough. It would never be enough for me. It hurt me intensely to think we would never have a baby.

After trying to conceive for two years, two years of having emotional breakdowns every month when that dreaded period arrived and two years of being able to focus on nothing else other than having a baby, we booked a doctor's appointment. Following our first appointment with the doctor the many tests began. A few issues were identified, and we were referred to the hospital. I attended several appointments and then we had a holiday, we had been through a tough couple of years in addition to trying for the baby and we needed a break. In hindsight, the 'tough' couple of years had caused such immense stress that it was likely a reason, if not the reason we couldn't get pregnant.

The week we came back from our holiday to Greece I was in work and I felt 'out of sorts', a bit lightheaded, tired, just not myself. I had a feeling I was pregnant. My period was only a few days late and this wasn't abnormal so desperately wishing I was but trying to manage myself for the disappointment, I stopped on my way home and got a pregnancy test. Weeks away from beginning our IVF journey I saw those two blue lines appear on the pregnancy test and I felt that gaping hole being filled instantly. I couldn't believe it was happening. I rang my husband who was working away after sending him a picture of the pregnancy test and we shared a fifteen-minute silent telephone call, we couldn't speak, every now and again one of us would say, "I can't believe it," and then silence.

I spent the months of my pregnancy watching my tummy grow, feeling the overwhelming love and excitement with every kick and movement that she made, obsessing over every detail, making sure everything was perfect for her to arrive. Months fantasizing over what she would look like, what she would be like, what colour hair she would have, what colour eyes she would have. I was the luckiest person alive; life would never be the same and we couldn't wait to meet her. Nine months of being in crazy, stupid, all-consuming love with my precious bundle of joy growing inside me.

The labour was traumatic, most are! I was advised at thirty-nine weeks to consider an induction due to reduced movements. Our girl was well and truly baked, and her long legs had run out of room in my tummy – I am four-foot-ten-inches and her daddy is six-foot-two so this was always a possibility. Three long days we spent on the induction ward, I felt like I had watched a million pregnant women come and go whilst we sat there waiting and waiting and waiting for our girl to make her appearance. On the third day she decided she was ready for this world – well ready to make a start anyway, she didn't arrive until day four.

After a very long labour I had to have an emergency caesarean. I can tell you that it really is an emergency; it took twenty minutes in total from the doctor making the decision to them laying me on the operating table. I can also tell you that your life really is in their hands. After being majorly dosed up on epidural so that the procedure can be undertaken you are asked to sign a piece of paper, literally signing your life away, you cannot read because you cannot see. You also cannot sign because your hands are numb and shaking. So, crying to my husband, telling him I couldn't see what the form said and genuinely frightened for my life (I wasn't selfish – they assured me that I was at risk but the baby was doing absolutely fine) I signed a signature as close to mine as my hands would allow and I prayed to whoever would listen to please keep us both safe.

The doctor promised me I would feel no pain during the surgery, he was not wrong. I did not feel any pain, what I did feel was as though someone was holding me off the floor by my stomach and shaking me as hard as they could from left to right. I had been given one tip from a friend when I was pregnant and that was, that if I did have to have a caesarean to not look at the light on the operating table because it is like watching the whole procedure in a mirror. I was so grateful for this advice, I kept my eyes closed and petrified, wished that it would all be over as quickly as possible.

You are not of sound mind from all of the drugs you have been filled with, but I was aware of when they had taken the baby out. I was also very aware that I had not heard a cry, scream...

nothing! I was also conscious that I had not seen my baby. I could tell from my husband's face that something was wrong. What is wrong with my baby? Why can't I hear my baby? I was asking these questions from the operating table. Delirious, hazy, shaking uncontrollably but I knew that something was wrong. I could feel it even on all of those drugs but I was still being operated on so I could not see what was happening. The anaesthetist came and sat next to me, she didn't say anything about my baby, she was just asking me if I was okay and explained what was happening to me. My husband was back and forth between the baby and I. His position far worse than mine, who should he be with? What could he tell his wife who was being sewn back together? He knew that our baby was not breathing, and I did not.

She did not breathe for herself for twenty-five minutes; those were the longest twenty-five minutes of our lives. Even though no one had told me, I knew! We were helpless in that situation, desperately hoping, praying, begging for her to breathe and be okay. The emotions were overwhelming particularly for my husband who was worrying over the lives of both his wife and his baby girl. I defy anyone who say men do not go through a labour like a woman, in that situation I would much rather have been me than my poor husband.

After the longest twenty-five minutes of our lives, we were handed our perfect baby girl. She was so beautiful; she was laid on my chest whilst I was on the operating table, our noses touching and her beautiful big eyes wide open peered into mine. I couldn't believe she was here, finally. Her eyes were so intense; she had the longest eyelashes, the most perfect eyebrows and a head full of black hair (explains the heartburn!). She was more perfect than I had ever imagined – though she did look just like my dad which was a bit weird!

To say we were slightly traumatised after the birth would be a massive understatement. It had frightened the life out of us. We couldn't talk about it, it was too emotional, too raw and too painful to relive. It took me a good year to be able to talk about the birth without finding it extremely distressing and emotional. I was once the biggest fan of 'One Born Every Minute', needless to say I have not watched this since my daughter was born. During our hospital stay I was moved to my own room, from my window I could see the maternity operating room, I knew it was that room from the surgery light. I sobbed for hours watching that light, reliving our traumatic experience over and over again!

I don't remember much else about the first twenty-four hours; I was filled with far too many drugs to remember. My husband did the first nappy and dressed our beautiful baby because I was pretty much stuck to one position having no feeling from the waist down. I was sad about this at the time, I always imagined we would do this bit together. I do have a memory of being hot, so hot and sweating, my whole body was itchy. Stupidly despite all of this I asked my mum to give me a bed bath and help me do my makeup, so I felt somewhat presentable for my visitors. I can assure you the makeup and bed bath did nothing for my image, absolutely nothing. It might have actually made me look worse – you know, like when you try to do your makeup on a hangover, and you get that look that's tired and people are unsure if you have done your makeup today or if it is the remnants of the night before. My stomach was still huge too, I didn't expect this, I obviously knew it would be big, but I wasn't prepared to still look as though I was carrying my baby!

Those first photos you see of mothers holding their newborns, wow I will never share mine, I look like death! About a week before our little beautiful baby was born, I had an eyebrow and eyelash tint and a lip wax so that I would look so natural yet so pretty in those first photos!

This is the level of planning that a naïve, clueless, first-time mama puts into her antenatal preparation.

I had a catheter for the first twenty-four hours. At the end of the twenty-four-hour period, the midwife came to remove my catheter and to help me walk to the toilet. I can tell you the first secret that no one had told me, the first wee. I can't be sure if this is just because I had a caesarean or if this is standard but they asked me to put a pan in the toilet so they could check my wee.

When I stood up, I screamed, I thought the surgeons had not put me back together properly. The pan was full of blood! And I mean full. I ran out of the toilet in a panic and collared the midwife, well actually and this is embarrassing to my coy self I collared a doctor and ordered him to get the midwife. He looked at me for a moment, a moment of hesitation until he must have realised that I was a crazy, fresh out of labour psycho and he followed my orders to get the midwife. Mortified on reflection! The midwife assured me this was normal. I made her come into the toilet and check, I could not believe that this was normal, I must not be explaining myself properly to her. She could not have understood the amount of blood that I was talking about! She looked, smiled, nodded and said yes totally normal. The relief, I had thought I was going to die right there on the spot when I saw that pan.

Day two – the pain! Wow! The pain was so intense; I was convinced I must have an infection, not a water infection I was convinced the wound had become infected, seriously infected that I was going to die because there is no way on this earth the pain should be that extreme. It throbbed. Any movement sending sharp stabbing pains and dull aches through your stomach. I could not believe that this was normal. Sneeze, cough or laugh, I beg you not to do this following a caesarean because the pain to that wound is unbearable. Unbearable yet you have to bear it because you have a tiny human to care for. The slightest movement would bring tears to my eyes, the movement that hurts the most is from a lie down to sit up position or a sit up to stand up position – of which you spend ninety percent of your day doing to get up to tend to your tiny. I looked and felt disgusting. My stomach was huge, my eyes were so dark, my head was foggy, so much was going on around us and I felt as though I was on another planet.

Due to complications during the labour, we were in hospital for a total of five days. These were to be the start of my longest and loneliest of days. I had never known what it felt to be surrounded by so many people, see so many familiar faces and feel so alone.

I had heard a few stories of baby blues and postnatal depression, but I had naively assumed this would pass me by. I see myself (or did see myself pre-baby) as a person who is head strong, a strong character, quietly confident, very laid back and passive (I am no longer this person – nearly there but not completely). I would be fine! Wow – I was so wrong. The first two days were a haze, I don't remember much, and I felt like I was floating on a cloud. The photo's my husband and I took in those first days are just that, photos, I cannot remember them being taken, I don't have a memory of those moments. It is weird to look back on these now. My husband refers to me as an elephant because I forget nothing but looking back at those photos is like looking at me living a life that was not mine. I have no memory or recollection; they are really just moments captured on a camera that have no place or time in my mind.

I must add here that since going through this, the term "baby blues" is far too underplayed. Baby blues has quite a nice ring to it I think, gives the impression that you might just be a little bit emotional. I took this term to mean that I might feel similar to what I would feel when I am due on, a bit emotional and very close to a temper tantrum on occasion. Baby blues should be called "head fuck situation". It quite literally refers to the fact that all of those pregnancy hormones that have been making you feel so wonderful, pink and fluffy about this pregnancy – particularly throughout your second trimester are going to leave your body, not gradually, not slowly but very fucking instantly.

I remember thinking what a chilled-out baby we had, she was so quiet, she hardly cried, hardly woke. This will be a piece of cake I thought – a passive, laid-back baby just like her mama (this was before I realised that there was a new version of me – anxious, chaotic and broken). What I didn't know was that my tiny was still full of all of the drugs that had been pumped into me during my labour! These would wear off just in time for day three!

Day three – bang… the "baby blues" (aka. head fuck situation) hit me and they hit me hard. I lied in that hospital bed when my husband left for the night and I cried, I sobbed, I pleaded for my old life, for this isolation and fear to go, for the pain to stop and to feel like me! I felt as though if I stopped concentrating on my next breath I would stop altogether, the scary part of this was that the thought of it was quite appealing. In that moment I felt like the most selfish bitch on earth. What was wrong with me? I had longed for this for years and here I was, ungrateful! This night was the night my baby girl started crying, she cried and cried and cried. I sat in my bed, and I cried with her. I was so frightened, so out of my depth, I did not know what to do.

A midwife came in to see if I needed anything, the room was in darkness, and I wiped the silent tears from my cheeks. She didn't say anything, she just told me to call her if I needed anything, I was so relieved and grateful – she did enough to acknowledge my upset without saying a word, knowing all too well I didn't want to utter a word of my feelings to her. My husband text to see if the baby had settled, no, is all I sent back and just like that he was back at the hospital. I was so pleased to see him. He called the midwife and asked her if we were doing something wrong (clueless, first timers), did the baby need something that we were not offering her. She said that my milk was coming in and that the baby could smell it, this would agitate her. She offered to take the baby for us so that we could try and get some sleep and she promised that when the baby needed us (feeding) she would bring her in and wake us. It was relief, pure relief. I was so thankful to her, to take that noise away and allow a couple of hours of much needed sleep.

I had my assessment with a midwife the next day, she asked about my mental health. I can't stop crying I told her, I didn't want to disclose my deepest darkest thoughts to her, I was so afraid she would think I couldn't cope and take my baby away from me. In those words, I realise just how irrational my mind was! I also realise now, that the overwhelming love and bond between mother and baby that I was not feeling must have been there, buried deep underneath that overwhelming fear but most definitely there. Why else would I have been so worried that they would take my baby away. The midwife told me it was normal; day three is when the baby blues hit you. You are exhausted and the baby is just starting to wake up.

I was trying to convince myself that I was okay, that I was normal, but I was worried. I didn't feel okay, I didn't feel myself,

I felt sad, upset, depressed!

I tried to reassure myself over and over again. Don't worry, you just need to get out of this hospital and get home with your baby and you will be fine. These feelings will go away. It's the hospital, that's all it is. These words were on repeat in my head over and over again.

When my husband came in the following morning, I told him I needed to get out of the hospital. I hated it. He took charge and spent the next two days upsetting many a midwife and doctor on his mission to free us from what felt like hell. I was frightened to hold my baby girl, change her, feed her, and bathe her in the hospital because I felt like I was being watched. Being observed as a novice first timer with no clue of what I was supposed to do or how I should do it. What if I did something wrong? The truth is no one was watching me; I was in my own room with very little attention from hospital staff. In that most vulnerable state, your body and mind exhausted you lose yourself and fear everything. I was so paranoid!

Day five – we were finally discharged! I walked out of that hospital thinking everything would go back to 'normal' now we were out of there. What I know now is that it was 'normal'; this was now our 'normal'. Life as we knew it had changed forever, but at that point I thought everything would be exactly as it was with the addition of a tiny human.

When I got home, I immediately wished I had stayed in hospital! Bloody ridiculous, isn't it? Laughable! At least there were medical professionals everywhere if something went wrong. I was paralysed with fear as soon as we walked through the front door.

My husband and I spent the next two weeks taking it in turns to watch and I mean watch our baby girl. We didn't leave her, not even for a second. I was so frightened that something awful was going to happen to her. In those moments I realised I did not have a fucking clue of what the hell I was doing. I was so sure I was going to break her. She was so fragile, so pure, and so perfect.

You have been preparing to bring your baby home for so long. You had imagined this magical moment of bringing them home and laying them so peacefully in the Moses basket or cuddling them up so small on the sofa. The reality is very different. You are so scared that you really don't know what to do. Your home now feels so scary. Even your mundane daily chores are gone by the wayside because the thought of leaving your tiny human to even boil the kettle seems like such a monstrous task and one that would require you to leave your tiny human for far too many minutes. I mean at this point there was no way I could take her into the kitchen, she had to be in the living room, there is no way I could pick her up and place her in another room! The fear was that real, the practical, logical; methodical me had lost all common sense. Of course you take your tiny human with you to do what you need to do. This thought, this obvious had passed me by and so I spent every hour of every day in the living room with her. The only place she was moved to was the bedroom when we went to bed hoping for some sleep!

So, now that you are finally home, this moment you have been so looking forward to – what do you do? After fumbling around the house like lost lambs we decided that we would just settle the baby and catch up on some of our programmes that we had missed whilst we were in hospital. Firstly, if you have recently become a mama, you will probably know by now that there is no such thing as settling a newborn baby. They are very much on their own schedule. You might think you have settled them, but they are just waiting for you to park your bum nicely on the sofa before all hell breaks loose and they scream the place down.

Nevertheless, once tiny human has you lulled into that false sense of security you get yourself comfortable, start your favourite programme and stare at the screen. That is all you do, either you do not have the mental capacity, or you have actually forgotten due to the intense fear of the situation you are in of exactly how a television works. You are mentally unable to focus on a picture and audio at the same time. I vividly remember taking three hours to watch the first half of '24 hours in Police Custody', at the end of which we both realised we had no idea what had happened during any of the programmes because we had stop/started it so many times and couldn't relax to take anything in anyway. I was in a state of no emotion, numb. It didn't bother me because I literally felt nothing, other than the overwhelming fear of course!

During the night feed I decided I would watch 'The Handmaid's Tale' I had loved the first series and in truth I was a sucker for anything sick, dark and twisted. I watched the first five minutes; nearly threw up, was petrified out of my mind and had to turn it off. I think that much darkness, blood and twisted shit was too much for me the mama who was currently traumatised by this tiny human and still massively struggling to deal with the trauma of the birth.

All I can say is that 'Love Island' was a godsend; it was the only programme I could watch and take in. So even if you hate reality TV, I promise you it is the perfect easy watch to teach you how to use a television again! The 2018 Islanders became my new best friends for my night time feeds. They stole my mind from my living nightmare for one hour a night and for that Islanders I am forever grateful!

Sleep – Sorry, What?

Sleep deprivation – once used as a form of torture! Sleep deprivation will quickly send your mind irrational, your thoughts dark, your sex drive non-existent and your general mental health in to utter despair. All the while you are responsible for a human life.

The sleepless nights – even a novice like me knew that this was a given with a newborn baby. This is what all parents DO tell you about when you are pregnant. Regardless of whether they have recently had a baby or had a baby thirty years ago, for everything they forget they do not forget the sleep, or lack of it!

I loved sleep! I say loved I probably still do but I can't allow myself to think too much about sleep. I say that as one of the extremely lucky ones who had a sleeper from about six weeks old (she rebelled against sleep when I went back to work, but I'll get to that). The pre baby me could quite easily spend a whole morning and a couple of hours into the afternoon of every weekend sleeping. I was well versed in a cheeky nap, some days if I felt tired in work and had plans afterwards, I would plan a quick twenty-minute pit stop at my house just to have a powernap. There was no such thing as too much sleep for me. In the week sleep was limited, I would and still do spend the hours of a school night that I should be sleeping binge watching the latest Netflix boxset or reading a book, promising myself that tomorrow I will get an early night. However, there was always a point in the week but most definitely on the weekend where I would indulge in those twelve hours of undisturbed sleep to catch up and recharge. The thought alone is heavenly.

When I reached the second trimester of pregnancy, I could not sleep. I'm not sure if it was pregnancy insomnia or just the total discomfort that would wake me, but it would not be unusual for me to be soaking in the bath at four a.m. and then waddling downstairs to watch TV or read a book. I was sure that my body was preparing me for the lack of sleep that was to be imposed on me as soon as my tiny human arrived. I had convinced myself so much that this was the reason for my inability to sleep that I was actually happy for the lack of sleep in pregnancy, because of course this would make it a piece of cake to handle when tiny human arrived! What an absolute dick – nothing can prepare you for newborn sleep deprivation!

NOTHING!

The sleep deprivation you experience in those first weeks and months (if you are one of the lucky ones it will only last this long) is indescribable. I can honestly say I have never experienced anything like it in my life, I wouldn't wish it on my worst enemy. That alone is enough to send you bat shit crazy without the added pressure of having to function enough to keep your tiny human alive. I have never felt anything like it. It physically hurt. I was sick to the stomach, it made me dizzy, my thoughts were dark – super dark! I would cry, I mean full on sob because I was so tired. I was frightened of how exhausted I felt, I would wake to my screaming baby and think I physically cannot do this. I was scared I would just fall asleep with her on me – sometimes I did!

I can vividly remember waking with a jolt in sheer panic because the baby was in my arms, I was feeding her and I had dropped off. It is a level of tiredness I have never even come close to feeling before. I used to think I was exhausted, that my working week drained me, but honestly – before this baby had arrived, I had experienced tiredness, never exhaustion. Sleep deprivation is the root of all evil, it is pure torture!

I was the lucky one; I only had to endure this intense level of exhaustion for six weeks. I was still extremely tired after this of course I was, I still am. The job of a mama never ends, even when your tiny human is tucked up asleep, HOPEFULLY for the night you don't rest. There are bottles to wash, cleaning to be done, the to do list is never ending and there is a level of worry that never goes away. In addition to the everlasting list of chores to be done if you don't steal an hour or two to yourself when they go to bed, then you literally have no 'me' time. Even if that 'me' time is enjoying the quiet because you really don't have the energy to do anything else. Even with a sleeper there are still restless nights and nights they just don't want to sleep so you can never be relaxed enough to 'switch off' till morning. How those mamas do this for the first few years I do not know. I bow to you; sincerely I do, because I struggle at least once a week with a sleeper, so to me you are a true legend, a living hero! How you function enough to keep your tiny human alive, let alone yourself no doubt your other half and go to work – you to me are superhuman.

Whilst we are on the topic of sleep deprivation and super humans we must talk about 'single mothers'. The only stigma surrounding 'single mothers' should be nothing but absolute admiration and respect. Those who are doing this on their own, with no 'other half' to offer any form of support, no cheeky lie in whilst the other takes over. They are the unsung heroes. They are doing the hardest job in the world – alone. The days your tiny human does nothing but cry and shout and whine, the days they are so poorly you cannot put them down, the days you are poorly but can't allow yourself to be unwell, the days you just want to run away for five peaceful minutes to yourself. Imagine those days where you have no one to turn to. These mamas still have to get up, get dressed, do the shopping, make the dinner, go to work – the difference being, they are doing this alone and not fucking moaning about it.

Sleep deprivation to them means just that, there is no one to take a turn so you can catch up on sleep. So, to any single mamas out there doing this alone, I salute you. You are the best there is!

When you have a sleeper you appreciate it, or I did, every day. I clearly remember that sleep deprivation and I know I am so lucky to be passed this phase. Well mostly passed this phase. Of course, there will always be disturbed nights – bad dreams, coughs, colds - mostly colds, babies get so many colds! One sleepless night makes everything seem so much harder, a week of them and I find my mood dip, that exhaustion seeping in, and I want to do absolutely nothing, other than lock us away from the world and nap all day. This only further highlights the total awe I have for those mamas still feeding through the nights, still awake playing at three a.m. and then making it to a baby class a few mornings a week fully made up and dressed. I mean, I simply would do nothing!

As your tiny human begins to creep through the months, they are far more active and mobile. A disturbed night to them now means that although they may be feeling so poorly it wakes them up and they cannot possibly go back to sleep, when you finally cave in and bring them downstairs in the hope that a quick nappy change and a bottle will send them back to sleep, they have other ideas. They now want to crawl around the house exploring absolutely everything that is a potential hazard, they definitely want to have a play, and you just have to read their favourite book to them fifty-five times and then, and only then, will they maybe consider going back to sleep. When they do drift off and you think bingo, don't be fooled into thinking you are now going to get those hours of beauty sleep in, the likelihood is they will wake within the hour, two if you're lucky, cranky as hell because they haven't had enough sleep and the person they will punish all day long is YOU, because it is obviously your fault, mama!

Sleep deprivation for me brought out the absolute worst in me. It made me so sad, irrational, angry, clumsy. It made me everything I thought I would never be when I became a mama.

The truth is, we need sleep and without it we are not ourselves. The emotions we feel are outside of our control until we can get our head down to try and have a decent sleep.

Everything is difficult when you're tired and a tired, cranky, demanding tiny human can quickly push you to breaking point.

The weird thing is, in those early days despite the sheer exhaustion I was so anxious that even though my tiny human quickly established a night-time routine I could not rest and relax when I went to bed. I was so fearful of her waking me with that painful scream I would sleep so lightly that I would hear every stir, every movement and every grunt that she made. I don't think that you can prepare, not fully prepare yourself for the level of absolute exhaustion that you feel, because unless you have been through it you do not know that this level of tiredness exists.

Of all the things I adjusted to as a mama, the parts of my life I have parked in my 'forgotten box' that I may eventually pick back up when she is older and much more independent, I will never get used to the lack of sleep. One bad night I can manage, two bad nights I can cope, three bad nights and I am miserable. Having said that for the first six months I went back to work my tiny human decided that a one a.m. wake up time was just perfect for her – I am not exaggerating. There were many days I went to work having slept from eleven p.m. to one a.m. – I did it, I don't know how, I think I fell into some kind of trance! It was hell – the weekend was when I would die, when I would allow myself to accept the tiredness.

From the age of one onwards, heed my advice – when that baby wakes do not take them out of their cot. If you do it once they know you will do it again. They will work all of their magic to get out of that cot, knowing that you will cave. Getting a baby back to sleep is one thing, getting a post-one-year-old back to sleep is near impossible if they have managed a few hours to raise their energy levels to one hundred percent whilst yours are dwindling somewhere around five. After finding out the hard way and caving just once, I then spent six months lying on my daughter's bedroom floor with my hand through her cot resting on her tummy. She spent most of those six months smacking me on the head, shouting, singing – she tried anything and everything to annoy me enough that I would cave once again and take her out of the cot. She did not win and eventually, persistent as she was, she realised her great efforts were getting her nowhere. She got bored of no response and after the longest six months I have ever lived (mostly awake) she decided it was probably best to just sleep through the night once more.

During your maternity leave there is the opportunity for a cheeky nap to be had whilst the baby sleeps, when you are working there is no such opportunity. You have to work like you don't have children and mother like you don't have work. My immediate work team were amazing, all mamas – they were so sympathetic and supportive of my situation. Outside of that as much as my colleagues and peers tried they just couldn't quite understand it. I would say the baby has been awake since one a.m. and they would say oh right, did you have to stay up with her? No, no I just let her downstairs and said I am popping back up for a sleep, babes, see you in a few hours – cereal in the cupboard, milk in the fridge. They meant well but just totally removed from my situation.

As awful as the sleep deprivation is – when you look back on those moments, those moments when you feel like you were the only two people awake in the world, they are some of my most special moments. Just think about it – in that moment when you believe you are the only two people awake in the whole wide world, there is suddenly no pressure. No pressure to have makeup on, no pressure to be dressed, no pressure to behave a certain way. No pressure – other than to just be. It's the perfect time to put on 'Secret Life of Pets' and eat crisps at two a.m. with your tiny because she wants crisps and chocolate and at two a.m. there is no routine, no rules and you are far too tired to negotiate or cut grapes in half for your almost-one-year-old. They are the special times, when you giggle with each other over something silly and lust after sleep with the knowledge that soon enough your tiny is going to need sleep too and whether you decide to snuggle on the sofa to snooze for as long as you can (because you will literally take anything right now), snuggle down in your bed or pop them in the cot and creep as quietly as you can to your own bed – in not so long from now when they sleep the night through only to wake up for school a tiny part of you might all of a sudden lust after those two a.m. wake up calls for crisps, chocolate and a movie!

The Screaming!

Reasons your tiny human will cry (SCREAM): - Milk, nappy, sleep, cuddle, too hot, too cold, bored, too light, too dark, over stimulated

Newborn babies scream! A lot!

Most of the time!

Crying – remove the association to a baby and what does crying mean? Crying is the response to being upset, distressed, in pain, frightened. So it is only natural that as a mama when you hear your tiny human crying you associate it with one or all of the above.

I wish I was the mama who didn't care what others thought. I never used to, but in a public place or in fact any place that had another human present (even family) my first thought was always the disruption my newborn was causing to others. On top of that was the thought that everyone was looking at me – the mama who had no clue what she was doing and could not console her baby. In my head this all translated to – everyone around you right now thinks you are a shit mama. Everyone knows you haven't got this and the most unrealistic mind-boggling shit in my head was that, this had never happened to any mama ever before. I honestly felt like I was the only mama in the world who had a baby that she could not console.

As a mama with a toddler now I realise that the reality is as follows; when a new baby cries my first thought is how warm my belly feels at the sound of a sweet little new born cry, my second thought is always of the poor mama who I hope is okay and not feeling under pressure, and my final thought is that I remember when that was me and I wish I could do it all again. Very quickly my mind is distracted, most likely by my strong-willed toddler throwing an almighty tantrum (which is definitely much more frowned upon by others than a helpless newborn) and I no longer hear that cute newborn cry, but I know for certain, that the mama can hear nothing but that cry.

To a mum, that cry, the cute newborn cry that everyone talks about, is piercing. It wrecks every nerve in your body. Your heart aches, you feel physically sick to the stomach and your anxiety level is through the roof. The noise only heightened by the fact that this poor tiny human cannot tell you what is wrong. In those early days you have so much to learn so you do what you have learnt so far. Your baby cries: you change their nappy, feed them, wind them and try to nurse them back to sleep. What happens though, when you have done all of the basics twice sometimes thrice and your tiny human continues to scream? I'll tell you what happens – you panic!

Desperately trying to figure out what is wrong, all the while the intensity of the scream is building. Your heart is racing and you're sweating! You feel like this screaming episode has been going on for hours, sometimes it has! When you reach this point, you will start to believe that something must be wrong with this baby. A few minutes longer and you are now certain that something is seriously wrong. You consider calling the doctors, out of hours, rushing them to A&E. In the earliest of days, you have not met your health visitor so really in these desperate times who do you call? I searched my discharge paperwork for a number, to who? Nanny McPhee? How could they let me take a human home and not give me a helpline? I have a helpline number when I buy a laptop but not a fucking baby. What the fuck do you do? You are that convinced by now, that there is no way on this earth your tiny human can be this distressed and not be dying. WRONG mama, they can be. It took me a long time to realise this. Too long!

This whole world is brand new to this tiny, fragile baby. They can't tell you if they're too hot, too cold, the lights are too bright, too dark, their clothes are itchy, they don't like the moses basket, the crib, the swing chair, the sofa, the floor, your arms – you get my drift! Everything is scary; they have lost the comfort of being inside your lovely, snuggly tummy, the luxury of having whatever they need at their disposal without needing to make a sound. Even understanding this in those early days doesn't always help. Exhaustion mixed with a screaming inconsolable baby is more than trying on many occasions!

In those early days when your tiny human is screaming and you have no idea why, because let's face it, why would you? You are basically strangers to one another, unable to communicate! In these moments you will look at your tiny human and you will beg them to tell you what is wrong, beg them to give you a sign, beg them to give you a clue, beg them to give you anything to let you know what is wrong and what you can do to help them.

Minutes of a baby screaming will feel like hours. In the nights it is even worse. Those nights are so long and so lonely. I longed in those dark lonely nights for someone to take her away. Awful is what you are thinking right? Writing it down makes it seem so much worse, but this was my truth, I could not handle this. More than not being able to handle this, I couldn't do this.

I did not feel that instant bond and overwhelming love that you hear mothers talk about. This frightened me immensely. Why didn't I feel it? Would I ever feel it? To me this tiny human was a stranger, a stranger that I was scared of, a stranger that I was longing to connect with but finding it so difficult to do so. I would stare at her for hours searching for that bond, that crazy all-consuming love. It wasn't coming. When I looked at her all I saw was fear. My fear. My overwhelming fear.

As the weeks passed us by these feelings were still prevalent and I started to worry that this was how it was going to be. That this was actually going to have an impact on her, as she got older. I worried that I would be a mother who would raise a child without much of a relationship and this terrified me. My mum has always been my best friend, for as long as I can remember, I assumed that I would be the same with my tiny human, the fact that I felt nothing but fear was petrifying me. Don't get me wrong as awful a person as I sound, I did care for her in the best way that I could. I made sure she was clean, I fed her, I tended to her and cuddled her when she cried. Each day I hoped it would come, I prayed that we would connect.

I realised in those first weeks that I was so much weaker than I thought. I always thought I was tough and could handle whatever life threw at me. The truth is, when things had got too tough or too much to bear in my life, I had removed them. If I didn't like a job, I had left and found a new one. If a relationship became strained or difficult, I ended it. If I found something uncomfortable, I just didn't do it. I wanted to leave this 'new life' in those moments, but I couldn't. I was stuck, I was trapped in what felt like hell.

Lonely. Vulnerable. Petrified. Anxious.

The whole time, I desperately wanted to enjoy these moments, but I hated every minute of them!

Our saving grace for the screaming baby was the bath. We must have had the cleanest baby on earth because she spent lots of time in that bath. One night the bath didn't work! We, being my husband and I, looked at each other in despair. Fuck, what do we do now!

She kept screaming. We were literally all out of ideas. After about an hour of trying to settle her in a million different ways and failing, I stood hopelessly in my kitchen, baby in my arms, tears streaming down my face and milk streaming from my boobs – yes this really does happen, my boobs quite literally wept with me! I had nothing left! In those moments you feel the lowest of low, you literally have nothing, no emotion, no energy, no hope! My husband came out the kitchen and took her from me. "I will try," he said. "Have a break, sort yourself out and have an hour to yourself."

By sort yourself out, I think he meant, have a shower and change your clothes you milk-leaking monster. Thirty minutes later, and that is being generous, it could have been five minutes, I was still stood in my kitchen, I think I was froze to the spot in fear. My husband reappeared with the still screaming baby in his arms. He had tears running down his face and he looked into my eyes and said, "I don't know what the fuck I'm doing." I was still crying and said, "Neither do I." We laughed, hysterically, over how pathetic we were. This tiny human had turned us into nervous wrecks and had us both (and my boobs) weeping in our kitchen! You must laugh at these moments; I think it is hysteria from the absolute fear and sleep deprivation but whatever it is – it helps!

When those episodes of screaming begin you approach each one trying to play it cool, thinking that this time might just be the time you can console that tiny human. You hope that this time is the time you can work out just what it is your tiny human wants. You think you got this, its fine they are just hungry. You prepare a bottle and feed them. The screaming continues, still fine, it's just wind, I've still got this. You wind your tiny human, and they continue to scream. Fuck, I totally haven't got this. The panic sets in, the fear, the irrational mind – oh God please someone tell me what is wrong with this baby. You are frantic now, you nurse them, sing to them, pat them, walk around the house with them, you try everything you have learnt so far. They are still screaming. Panic mode is in full swing, the sweating is underway, and you are shitting yourself.

Once you have passed all of those stages you get to the worst stage of all, you get angry. Admitting this now is hard, but emotionally it was where I got to on many occasions. I would start saying to my tiny human things like; what is wrong with you? What the hell is wrong with you? Stop crying! Please stop crying! The panic within you is causing the anger, at the time you feel like the worse mama in the world, you know that anger is definitely not the right response here but managing your emotions is totally beyond your control right now.

At some point in that awful moment of anger there is a pause in that screaming. It is at this point you look at their beautiful, perfect face whilst they rest peacefully in your arms, and you feel like the worst human in the world. You can't believe the anger you felt only five minutes ago, this is so out of character for you.

If this resonates, fear not, this does not make you a bad mama. You will feel like shit about it, that alone is enough to tell you that you are only human and most likely a sleep-deprived human too. As quick as that you compose yourself and you tend to your tiny human with nothing but love and probably a lot of guilt.

When I look back at the early days this is the only thing I regret. The fear and not enjoying it is not something I will regret, I could not help how I felt and although I did not enjoy those early days I did do my best to care for her. The anger though, I definitely regret this.

My health visitor told me on her first visit that if you have tried everything and your baby is still crying, put them down in a safe place for five minutes and walk away. Breathe, take those five minutes to compose yourself and then go back to your baby and try again. She told me this in the first week of being home from hospital and I thought what a crazy woman, what the hell is she talking about, as if I would need time to compose myself. That advice is so important, I beg you to take it and use it in those trying moments. You are a better mama when you return to tend to your tiny human after those five minutes and the likelihood is that you will settle your baby. They won't be burdened by a tense mama but will be comforted by a relaxed one.

You are also given the advice from your health visitor and others around you to sleep when the baby sleeps. This is shit advice – well it was for my first baby, if I was ever lucky enough to do it again then I would definitely steal as many of those precious naps as I could! I was so anxious of the screaming when my tiny woke that I used to sit and watch her sleep. The thought of waking to that scream was too much for my fragile state to handle. I would sit and watch her, wait for the stir, the tiniest movement before bombing to the kitchen to make a bottle. I spent my night making bottles and then throwing them away two hours later because it really was only a stir and she had continued to sleep away peacefully!

The ten minutes it took me to make a bottle and then cool it down felt like ten hours when she was awake, she screamed the whole time! I would try anything and everything in those ten minutes to stop the crying – a dummy, singing to her, the swing chair, nursing her, rocking her. Nothing worked! All she wanted was that bottle and I had no way of explaining to her that it was on its way, that I wasn't an evil bottle depriving mama, I was just cooling it so that it didn't burn her tiny tongue.

The anxiety at every bottle time did not ease. I fed on demand for far too long and therefore I was never prepared, I never had a bottle ready at the exact time she needed it. Watch for the cues people said, there were no cues, my tiny human would open her eyes and scream the fucking place down – that was my cue! I had been advised by the midwives and my health visitor to feed on demand, what my naive self didn't know was that at some point you have to stop feeding on demand and establish a routine. Why would I know this? I had never had a baby before!

I urge any expectant mother to spend the eighty pounds, or however much it is and buy a 'Perfect Prep' machine. It would not be a waste of money. I thought I had everything I possibly needed for this baby but in hindsight this machine was the only thing I needed and the only thing I didn't have!

My friend saved me from my despair when my baby girl was twelve weeks old. She came to visit us and was feeding her son of the same age three hourly, the very next day we started the same routine. This made such a massive difference to the both of us, I was always prepared and the screaming for bottles was over! My anxiety was slowly easing, and I felt such a sense of relief and freedom.

In those early days you will do anything within your power to prevent that baby from crying, and I mean anything.

This even applies to how you dress your tiny human. Remember all of those beautiful clothes you filled your baby's wardrobe with when you were pregnant? If you are a loser like me, you will have washed them, hung those tiny garments on the washing line to dry – taken a photo because they looked so damn cute and then put them so carefully away in the tiny wardrobe. You will probably take just one more photo of their clothes so neatly lined in their wardrobe because why wouldn't you! Just to add a note here, once baby is here you never hang washing that neatly on the line, there isn't the time! Their wardrobe – you never look inside that, not until they are about four months old because you just don't have the time, you just pop your hand in, grab anything that feels slightly like a babygrow and do the tenth outfit change of the day.

Once tiny human arrives, those teeny tiny, cute garments remain on hangers in their wardrobe and you dress them in nothing but vests and babygrows. You do this for two reasons, the first being you are petrified you may actually break them because they are so fragile – or so you think, and secondly because you are doing anything to reduce the amount of screaming. Dressing them in these cute but very impractical garments is not going to help with this, so you just don't bother. On that special occasion where you brave a new outfit, they wear it for all of an hour, you make the most of a photo opportunity by which point they have probably leaked through their nappy and are covered in pee or poop so you peel it off them and reach for the trusted babygrow. By the time you are confident enough to take a step up from the babygrow, you manage to fit them into ALL of their new outfits in a week, you are literally squeezing them into them because if you are honest, they have already outgrown the newborn size. They really do grow that quickly!

Here's another one I was told by many: babies have different cries and you mama will know what each cry means. Have you heard this? I kept hearing this in my first weeks as a mama and I was thinking great just another thing to add to my shit list. If there was one thing I was sure of in those early days was that when my baby girl was crying, I never knew what she was crying for.

There was just one cry, well, scream. It sounded the same every time! There was no difference in her cries. I was listening, watching, reverting back to my Dr Google research – they were definitely all the same. So, I'm here to tell you mama that there IS only one bloody cry. I had obsessed over this cry theory for months!! I had started to believe that the overwhelming fear and the terrible thoughts I had in those early days had damaged my tiny human and as a result of my emotions and feelings she was unable to communicate with me through her cries.

I mean, just read that back, that really is pathetic, it should give you an insight in to how crazy my once sane mind had become. It is ridiculous how self-critical you become when you become a mama. You turn into a worrier, even if you considered yourself a worrier pre-baby this is a whole new level, the word worry carries a whole new meaning. You are unbelievably irrational. Sleep deprivation and hormones are the recipe for an irrational first time mama, creating constant despair, panic and worry.

The different cries are a thing, but they didn't appear until my tiny human was about six months old. From six months old, the cries are definitely different, and you will know whether your tiny human is hungry, tired, bored, in pain - whatever the problem is you will know. It would be a million times more helpful if these cries did appear from newborn, by six months you have generally figured each other out, you likely have a routine and the crying by now is far less frequent and easily consolable.

So, we have established that the crying/screaming is horrific. The only certainty of a newborn is that they will cry – a lot, it is the only way they are able to communicate at this point. Keep strong now, mama! Aim for week seven, the screaming doesn't stop here but it definitely lessens. It really does peak at week six; you believe that this has actually got worse – well for that week at least it has. Tiny human has ramped it up and you lose any confidence you had started to rebuild, you fear that you have gone back to square one, worse than square one actually because the screaming really is that bad. Just get through the dreaded week six. Prepare yourself for the peak of screaming and sit tight. Week seven arrives, and your baby will literally change overnight, you realise at the end of your first day that you are able to count the number of times your baby has screamed! This is a major improvement, a massive step forward – this is progress! You've made it through the worst. It is still hard, well it was for me, but with the screaming having eased you realise you can actually start to breathe, start to think, stop living entirely on those nerves.

Well done, mama – you're almost there now!

Babies Sleep When They Are Tired!

If your baby becomes overtired, it is hard to get them to sleep. If you are lucky enough to get an overtired baby to fall asleep do not fool yourself in to believing you are a rock star and have just bagged yourself a nice couple of hours to yourself. An overtired baby will likely wake up soon after they have fallen asleep. Newsflash – did you know there are actually limits to how long your baby should be awake?

WRONG!

When I was pregnant it had never crossed my mind that I would need to help my baby sleep. I know what you are thinking, what did actually cross my pregnant self's mind? I thought newborn sleep was a given. All of those precious pictures of sleeping babies that I had seen before becoming a mama were clearly just false advertising, or a result of parents only being able to take a photo when tiny human sleeps because it is the only time they are not screaming!

I assumed, wrongly, that when babies are tired, they fall asleep, you know, just nod off. How wrong was I? When I was wearing those rose-tinted glasses in pregnancy, I had thought that newborn babies sleep most of the time. I imagined hours of peace, hours to recover, hours to lounge on the sofa watching telly with tiny human snuggled up peacefully on my chest. If only the pregnant me knew how far off I was from reality.

When my tiny human was about three weeks old, I realised

that she was spending a lot of time awake, sometimes five hours at a time. When your baby is mostly screaming then, five hours feels like a week! This didn't feel right to me, I mean, I knew nothing about babies clearly but even for a novice I felt that this was wrong. Why is she always awake?

As always, I turned to Dr Google for some advice. I was shocked, from birth to six weeks a baby should be awake for no longer than one hour before they need a nap. I read on and learnt that you need to help your newborn go to sleep before they become over stimulated or over tired. What? Are you kidding me? What the hell did this mean?

Anyway, as I continued to read on, I learnt that too much light, TV, noise etc. could over stimulate your baby, which means that when they are tired and want to sleep they physically can't. Thank you, Dr Google, I was now an educated mama on sleep - do not over stimulate baby, after forty-five minutes begin to try and get your tiny human to sleep. Brace yourself, baby girl, mama has learnt something new, and you are now going to sleep like a newborn baby.

Perhaps I should have mentioned earlier, that whilst I was clearly, absolutely ill prepared for the life changing event that was about to happen to me when I brought this perfect tiny into the world (as you can tell from the read so far) I am good at a bit of research. If I have a problem, I will research it until I am an expert. Yes, I should have done this before the baby arrived, granted, but I was enjoying my pink and fluffy pregnancy with all of my unrealistic expectations and ideas of what having a baby actually meant in reality. So, following the arrival of the utter chaos my life had become, I googled every issue. Learnt it inside out and back to front, took some mental notes of the remedy and put that into practice with my newborn. How my mama or any mama before our generation got through the baby phase without google is beyond me.

Easier said than done! Even after me becoming a sleep expert for newborns thanks to Dr Google – still, she would not sleep. I would sit in my living room with the curtains drawn, TV off, lights off, silence but still she would not sleep. There was nothing that would make this baby sleep in the day. Hours of rocking her back and forth, singing to her, shushing her, stroking her face, lying her in her cot, walking her round the block, playing her white noise. You name it, I tried it, she just could not sleep. Sometimes if I was lucky, she would fall asleep on her bottle, now I know that is frowned upon by many professional but trust me I did not care. If it wasn't for those bottles, sometimes I think she would have stayed awake all day long.

The car was a joke! Take her for a drive and she would fall asleep in the car, are you joking me? Have you heard this bullshit? I heard that all the time. My baby girl hated the car. She would scream from the moment we got in the car until the moment we got out, including when someone sat in the back with her. If I was driving alone, many times I had to pull over because she had got herself in such a frenzy she would be gasping for breath. A personal highlight of me rocking motherhood involved me doing a wheel spinning emergency stop onto a lovely person's gorgeous drive in one of the poshest areas of Cardiff in sheer panic because my tiny human had screamed so much she was hyperventilating. I pulled my tiny out of the car and cuddled her so tightly and rocked her to ease her car distress. The very lovely, very well-spoken owner of said house walked out to his drive to ask if I was okay. I frantically explained that my daughter does not like the car, and she is very distressed, he was very kind to me – on reflection I probably looked a bit crazy and all the while

I was oblivious to the fact that I had just bombed onto his drive. To summarise, my tiny absolutely hated the car. She never fell asleep, she just screamed. I was all out of ideas.

Your tiny human is screaming, you know that they are tired, you have tried everything to help them sleep yet they continue to scream. They are red in the face and by now you are of a similar colour, you are staring at them, all out of ideas, willing them to just fall asleep. The whole time thinking, I would do literally anything to sleep right now.

You try reasoning and negotiating with tiny human. When you are exhausted from trying, exhausted from the screaming and feel as though you have nothing left to give you will on many occasions find yourself trying to reason and negotiate with a tiny human who has no fucking clue of what you are saying.

"You are tired, baby, that is all that is wrong with you. If you go to sleep now you will feel so much better when you wake. Please baby, just go to sleep." I mean what are you hoping is going to happen here?

Do you think they will just say, "Okay, mama, thanks for letting me know, I have been wondering what the problem is here, I will just close my eyes and drift off now…" – if only!

When my tiny human was about six weeks old, my cousin who had recently had a baby came over, my baby was screaming as she mostly did. "What is wrong with her?" she asked (she had one of those babies who didn't cry, fell asleep when she was tired and was generally chilled most of the time).

"I don't know," I said. "I think she is tired. She definitely can't be hungry, her nappies just been changed and I'm pretty sure she has no wind."

"Wow," was her response. She could not believe she would be in this state because she was tired. "I'll have her, you make us a coffee," she said.

After about ten minutes there was silence, I couldn't believe it! I didn't want to look! What had happened? Why had the screaming stopped? I ever so slowly walked into my living room just as she was laying my baby girl down in her moses basket, FAST ASLEEP! "How did you do that? What are you?" Then she showed me a trick that would save me in my future weeks and months. She had stroked her face from the top of her forehead to the tip of her little button nose repeatedly and she had fallen asleep in her arms. Since I learnt this trick, this well-kept secret I have seen loads of mamas doing this to their tiny humans. Was I always that person who wanted a baby with little to no interest in other people's babies? That must have been the case, my friends all had babies, there were always babies around me – I noticed every single one of those babies when I was desperately trying to get pregnant, but I had never noticed this best kept secret! Or perhaps, before you're a mama you see these things, but you don't notice them. They are insignificant before you 'get it'.

Anyway, following my genius cousin's advice, I was sceptical, but with no better ideas and no success on the sleeping front in previous weeks I braced myself for the next nap time. I rocked her gently in my arms and stroked her from her forehead to the tip of her nose and… she fell asleep in my arms! I wanted to cry. This woman needs an award! I felt as though I owed her money, I could not believe it. This little gem of a trick worked for us *almost* every time. Until she got to around six months old, then she was a bit cuter and this trick was responded to with her clapping her hands. But by six months you will totally have this, even if the sleep time in the day is a battle that will be your only battle most days so it will be no big deal. Re-phrase, unless you're exhausted and then everything is a big deal!

What my baby girl was always good at though (as disclosed before, minus the six month hiccup when I went back to work) was sleeping through the night. I assume this must be a fluke, luck of the drawer, I don't know. But I can tell you what I did and maybe it will help. I hope it does if you don't have a sleeper because sleep deprivation on top of everything else you are going through right now is a killer!

In the first two weeks I breastfed, this meant my baby girl was feeding from me hourly and it was awful. I have never experienced tiredness like it, I was beyond tired I couldn't think straight, couldn't see straight or even walk straight for that matter. After two weeks she refused to take from me and I moved her to formula. I struggled to take the leap initially, which was strange. When I was pregnant my response to the bottle or breast question was always, "I will try my best but I'm not precious about it. If it doesn't work, I'll give a bottle, food is food." Yet two weeks in, the sleep deprived, irrational 'new' me found the transition immensely painful. I felt guilt, I felt I had failed as a mama but after some convincing by my husband and mum I gave her a bottle. The relief! Oh my God, the relief! As awful as that may sound to some, I was so relieved. I could now share the feeds and the pressure I had felt to ensure my baby was getting enough milk from me and my absolutely tiny boobs was over, it had been immense. As soon as I gave her the bottle, she would feed two-hourly in the day but four-hourly in the night, I was in heaven!!

From this point I established a bedtime routine. I have always been a bit of a nerd when it comes to routines and planning. I would bathe her around six-thirty p.m.; give her a baby massage (at this point, I just made this up, it wasn't a researched massage), feed her and then put her to bed around seven-thirty. In the early days bed was a sleepyhead in the living room, she loved it more than anything else and it was easy to transfer her to the next to me crib when we went up to bed. We did this every night until she was six months old, from six months old bedtime meant up to her bedroom to sleep in her cot.

I do recognise though that we are the lucky ones, we are blessed that she slept well. My husband is convinced it is because I set her a routine and stuck to it, I am not so convinced. I think we were just blessed with a sleeper but it's worth a shot if you are having sleepless nights and haven't tried this already. Though please don't mistake me for an advice giver, I will share what I did but I am no expert despite the fantastic relationship I developed with Dr Google.

My tiny human was always keeping us on our toes, always moving the goal posts. She would go through phases of liking and disliking different comforts. At first, she wouldn't settle in the moses basket, then she loved it. The same applied to the crib, the beanbag and almost all of the general baby items we had for her. So, what I am saying is, don't try once and give up. Keep trying, persevering, they are changing all the time.

A little tip here, mama, if you are lucky enough to have a sleeper don't forget those mamas around you who are doomed with a baby who does not yet know that night and day exist. Do not brag! Do not be one of those mamas! The worst thing a sleep-deprived mama can hear right now, is how wonderfully your baby sleeps through the night. I mean if you are one of the lucky ones imagine those poor mamas who are six months in and still feeding two-hourly through the night. They do not want to hear how you are having a wonderful, luscious twelve hours a night.

One of my mama friends was still on two-hourly feeds at eight months old, she handled it like a true pro but honestly when she would ask me how my baby girl slept, I wanted the floor to swallow me whole. I actually felt like the shittiest person on earth telling her that she slept through the night. I played it down and moved the conversation swiftly on! Sleep deprivation for that long is horrific, I don't know how she did it, but I do know that she is a better person than me to be able to function and look great on such little sleep.

Acceptance for me was key. Though still absolutely exhausted EVERY day of my entire life as a parent, once I accepted that the sleep I once knew and loved was part of that selfish life I once lived and loved, it became much easier to deal with. Your sleep, just like your life will never be the same again. Well, maybe it will one day but for now you need to lock it in that box of luxuries to forget.

Leaving the House!

One of the most daunting thoughts is to step outside of those claustrophobic but oh so comforting four walls. The most daunting but probably the most necessary to try and hold on to your sanity.

After spending too many hours in the same four walls trying to figure out what the fuck is happening, cabin fever will set in. You may even start to resent your home, for me I began to associate it with the anxiety I was desperately struggling with. However, even though those four walls are closing in on you, the thought of leaving the security you feel in your own home is nothing short of terrifying. Until this point when your tiny human screams for a whole hour and you cannot console them, apart from possibly your neighbours, nobody is there to witness the noise, the distress and the fact that you have absolutely zero clue of what to do.

Going out for food and enjoying a glass of wine or ten, knowing you have no washing up to do after a meal was our favourite thing to do before our tiny human arrived. This wouldn't need to change once our baby was here, we would just take her along with us. We will keep our lives just as they were, and she will just come along with us. Fools! We genuinely believed this would be our truth.

Ironically, these were often our conversations whilst we were enjoying a delicious meal in one of our many favourite restaurants when I was pregnant. Where it was obligatory to order and clean every plate of a three-course meal – this is poignant. Once tiny human arrives you will quickly realise that you are lucky to have one course a day at first and if you do manage that course, you won't enjoy it. Eating becomes a self-set challenge of how much you can get from your plate to your grumbling, aching stomach and how quickly you can do this.

We thought we would 'have' this from the beginning; it would be a breeze. All of these people who change their lives for the sake of a baby were idiots. I mean, why would you allow a tiny human to dictate to you what you did and when. Writing this now our tiny human is here and has completely taken over our lives and dictates exactly what we do and when is hysterical – we were the idiots! We were so narrow minded and naive as to what was about to happen to our lives, to us. The truth is nobody 'has' this as a first-time parent. You're not supposed to 'have' this, you're supposed to just survive, just get through the shit storm for the first few months until you finally start to find your feet and come somewhere close to 'having' this.

This tiny human was about to rock up and create the biggest shit storm we had ever known, and we had absolutely no idea. When you hear people say, I miss being pregnant, and you think, really Karen because you moaned the whole fucking time. What they mean is they miss the quiet, they miss the calm, they miss their life. They miss caring for this tiny human when they were unable to scream the fucking place down.

So, we are about two weeks in now and we go out for some food. It takes us literally all day, and that is no exaggeration, to get her and ourselves ready. The mammoth task of packing her bag and getting her safely into her car seat and we are off. I promise you, the bag packing gets easier, practice makes perfect. Soon ten bags become one and then one becomes a small, cute bag that means the handbag you stashed away many months ago can become that lovely thing you carry on your arm once again. Anyway, we get to the restaurant, and she is asleep – perfect, we think, because in truth we are petrified of her when she is awake. The bottle is at the ready just in case!

Very early on in your new role as mama you will master the skill of inhaling your food. If you haven't mastered this skill yet, waste no time and get practicing because if you don't you will actually starve! I order a glass of wine with my meal, my first since before I was pregnant, believing that it might help me to relax a bit and enjoy my first meal out. It did not, if anything it just heightened my anxiety! I spent the whole time watching my tiny human, petrified that she would wake. She stirred, we got the bill and left. I actually left half a glass of wine and I NEVER leave wine! At least we made it out.

After having a successful meal out the first time and I mean that genuinely – we did manage to eat; we had become lulled into that false sense of security these tiny humans impose on us. We thought, we totally got this and so we did it again a few days later. It was a disaster. Our tiny human woke as soon as food came, we gave her a bottle and she screamed, and screamed and screamed some more. My husband and I gave our best efforts at trying to console her, of course without success. In that moment you feel like the entire restaurant is staring at you, eyes burning through you willing you to shut that baby up. You sweat, you're scared, you're pissed off because you really wanted this to be a nice thing to have done together and you want to cry.

We took it in turns to take our beautiful but very noisy baby outside and walk her in the pushchair, we realise that not everyone wants to hear a screaming baby when they are trying to enjoy their meal. We were one of those couples before who would wince at the sight of a baby on the next table when we were hoping for a romantic meal together. What this ultimately meant was that we spent the entire time on our own. There is nothing more depressing than hastily eating a meal in a restaurant whilst anxiously watching your husband walk up and down willing that baby to sleep. You do not taste your food, you don't even want it, you just want to gather your things and leave – crying!

That was it for us, we would just have to stay in now. We would just have to stay in our house forever! What was the point in going out? I mean, staying in is depressing enough but at least we could do it together in the privacy of our own home. Without worrying about all those people peering at you thinking you have no clue what you are doing. We already know people, we totally haven't got this, and you are absolutely right, we have no fucking clue of what we are doing!

I mention that we are two weeks in. If your baby hasn't been born yet you may be thinking, it's only been two weeks! However, at two weeks in, your mind is already irrational. Two weeks of overwhelming fear that has remained prevalent and constant and two weeks of sleep deprivation makes you feel as though you've been in this situation for at least six months.

The problem is, if you respond in that way, in the way that we did then you become even more insular, which is not a good place to be in your anxious, vulnerable state. So, with the confidence once again crushed instead of trying to go out for food or to any public place ever again I decided that I would just take her out for walks. Walks were safe space.

You've spent months of your pregnancy contemplating what pushchair to buy from the vast selection available. You choose a pushchair that you have fallen in love with and then you picture yourself dressing your baby, laying them in the bassinette and walking to your local shops, the park, café, anywhere just to show off your bundle of joy. When that time comes the weirdest thing happens, you are too bloody frightened to leave the house with tiny human on your own, pushing a pushchair. What if they wake and cry? You already know without any uncertainty that ninety-nine percent of the time you cannot console them, so really what will you do?

I will tell you what you will do. You will spend an hour trying to get your tiny human to sleep, you will place them ever so gently in the bassinette and then you will walk as fast as you possibly can stopping in absolutely no shops, cafes or restaurants whatsoever just in case they wake. When they wake and that dreaded screaming begins you will learn to walk faster than you ever thought humanly possible to get them home. If you have had a caesarean then the heightened pace of the walk pains your wound, the dullest ache through your stomach that will last for the rest of the day. Six weeks, you are expected not to do anything too strenuous (like raising a newborn?) and not to drive. What they didn't say was, don't run as fast as your legs will take you, whilst negotiating a pushchair that carries your most precious possession.

So, at this point you're too scared to stay home and too scared to go out! You think you're going crazy (on reflection and reading this back, I was crazy) and you feel like a total failure. Why can't I do this? I was watching other mothers doing this effortlessly, in my eyes no one else was struggling the way that I was. I had seen mothers doing this; they totally 'had' this. Chilled out happy babies with chilled out happy mamas were out there. I felt as though it was me, it was just me, I couldn't do this. I didn't want to do this!

"Get out," people say. "It will do you both good," they say.

Really? Will it really do my nerves any good? How about my crippling anxiety? And don't forget my outrageous fear, will it ease that? I believe not! I do keep trying though, because I know I have to. What's the alternative? Lock yourself away? This was not a bad idea, this did cross my mind, this did seem so appealing. For me though, I wasn't that person before, and I didn't want to become that person now. More than that, I didn't want those around me to know that I wasn't coping. So eventually a walk around the block turned into a walk around the park and then if she was asleep a quick visit to the shop. Slowly but surely, it was the tiniest bit of progress but at least we are getting out of the house, if only for a walk!

The most annoying part of this is that you want to be out; you want to visit friends, family and meet other mums. Whilst you were pregnant you spent hours imagining how you would spend your days on maternity leave; visiting the shops, sitting down to order a nice drink and a sandwich for lunch, reading your book in the park whilst cuddling your newborn. All of those unrealistic daydreams. Locking yourself away from the world, hiding in constant fear every day never entered your mind.

To any mama feeling this way, stop beating yourself up, stop being so hard on yourself.

This is still brand new to both of you, you are both learning. You are both finding each other. It is still such early days at this point and there is absolutely no rush. In a few months' time you will find that it is actually easier to be out of the house than it is to stay in. By that point your tiny human will be so curious and nosey that they will be bored of being at home. So, if you want to spend many of your first days and weeks inside then do it!

Soon enough those days will be over, and you will wish you had made the most of them.

If you plan to return to work after your maternity leave and find yourself battling your way through what feels like hell, then use this as a tool to help you. Use this timeline as your focus. Try to enjoy something from each day to begin with, even the melt downs, if only so you can lay with your baby, cuddle them so tightly and take in their beautiful baby smell.

The washing can wait, the cleaning can wait, the shopping can wait – but I promise you mama, that baby won't wait. They will soon be grown, and these days will be nothing but a distant (and fond) memory. To help me embrace those precious moments, even on the most trying of days I started to imagine myself one year later sat at my desk in the office, it is only then that I would wish for those moments all over again – and I do, every day!

Don't get me wrong, there are some days I long for her bedtime, some days where nothing is good enough. I have not turned into one of those mamas that lie to you and tell you they love every single moment. It is sweet heavenly bliss. That is bullshit, some days are shit, really shit and on those days, I would look forward to going back to work but as the months go by those days of wishing for work become few and far between.

I cancelled so many meet ups in those early days, arranged with such good intentions and then feeling far too frightened on the day. I was embarrassed. Embarrassed, that I could not console my own baby. I wanted other mums, especially those who knew me before I had a baby to think I had this, to think I was a natural. In addition to this, I had the constant shame of having been so desperate for this for so long. Those close to me knew this, they had been on this journey with us and here I was, doing what felt like, a pretty shitty job in my new role as mama.

Those who knew me before knew how I was as a person, knew how I liked to have things in order and be in control of my own shit. What would they think of me now? I could not hold a conversation; I was so scared all of the time that I could not focus my mind on anything. I found no enjoyment whatsoever in meeting friends for food or coffee, for one I could not eat or drink with a screaming baby in my arms and secondly, it was far too overwhelming to have every pair of eyes in that restaurant or café staring at you in sheer disgust whilst your tiny human screamed so loud anyone would think I had punched her in the face!

What I see now that I couldn't see then, was that those people who are your friends only want to support you. If they have children of their own, they know. They have been there; they are not phased in the same way that you are by that screaming. I also know that for every disapproving look you get when you are out, and your tiny human is screaming with not a thing in the world that will console them there is another mama who is looking at you with heartfelt understanding. They are thinking, 'I feel for you, mama.' If they are normally the ones trying to deal with a meltdown they are thinking, 'Thank God it's not me!'

Either way, hold your head up high and think, 'Fuck the lot of you, what do you expect me to do? You have about as much control over this tiny human as I do and trust me disapproving people, I would do anything to stop this baby screaming right now, ANYTHING!'

Whether I was going out, having a visit from the midwife, the health visitor or someone who I would call my nearest and dearest, I did everything in my power to try and get my baby girl to sleep ahead of the event in those early days. The thought of those I knew, or strangers witnessing the fact that I could not do this, I could not cope with this was far too painful for me to experience again. So, staying in or going out I would plan my whole day around trying to get her to sleep, ready for whatever it was we were doing.

I vividly remember the midwife coming to visit us when my tiny human was around ten days old, she was asleep just in time for her arrival. "Wow, she is so content, is she always like this?" I lied, of course I lied.

"Yes," I said. Then she got out the weighing scales, why? Why on earth would you do this to me? Why would you force me to wake my tiny human when I have just spent the last hour and a half getting her to sleep? Dread, fear, panic seeped through me. If you have had your baby by now then you will know that those scales signal a time to strip your baby off, completely starkers and lay them on to the weighing scale. When you have just spent all morning getting your baby to sleep for this specific visit then all that means is the screaming is going to be so much worse than if you had just braved it and kept them awake for the visit. Imagine being woken up by being stripped off and led in a weighing scale – I would probably scream the place down too!

I wish I had been honest with my midwife and my health visitor, I know from my mama friends now that they are so supportive to those of us who are struggling. Hindsight is a great thing. Don't be shy, mama; if it is all going to shit, tell them. Tell them it's shit, tell them you are struggling, tell them you can't cope, they are there to help you. I wish I could have been more honest because if you pretend all is well, they will leave you to your own devices. Their time is needed for those mamas who are being honest, who are opening up about their melt downs, their anxiety, their fear. I know this because I have watched the support a loved one has received following her honesty. Her health visitor was wonderful, so caring, so supportive and most importantly she was there, a lot.

I feared always, that if they thought I couldn't cope then they would take my baby away. I know now that this was all in my head, I had lost myself and all rationale completely along this journey. Whilst some people around me knew I was finding it hard I don't think many of them knew I was completely and utterly broken. I was doing everything that I needed to be doing, everything that a newborn needs. Full of fear, anxiety and a total lack of confidence or self-worth, quite definitely, but I was still doing it.

If I could do it again, I wouldn't rush myself to do anything. I wish I had enjoyed more time snuggled on the sofa, more time in my pyjamas, more time not doing my makeup and getting dressed in those earliest of days. Feeling like I had to put on a front caused damage. In all of this I had forgotten how to relax, I could not sit until everything was done and even then, I was thinking of the next thing that needed doing. In amongst it all I had forgotten me. That was fine for that moment, but it was damaging and it took a lot of work and a lot of time to repair myself. If I were to do this again, I would relax more and maybe just maybe my baby would relax more too. Enjoy the home comforts, the not needing to be anywhere, no pressure of work and nursery and life! Once you go back to work (if you do) the business of life takes on a whole new meaning. Most of the week is spent rushing from one place to another, you finally understand the meaning of 'life passing you by', so don't feel like you have to get out. Take your time and enjoy those precious moments, embrace them all because life will be busy again soon, really busy.

When you have a baby the decisions you make are not focused around you anymore, there is a shift, decisions are made with your family at the forefront of your mind. This is the time to exercise your new power as a mama, where you make 'selfish' decisions, those best for your family, you are allowed to say no guilt free because 'it's not right for the baby'. When someone tells you to start getting you and the baby out, it will do you good tell them to go fuck themselves. Unless of course you feel you are ready. The advice they give is always with the best intention I know, but honestly what are you getting out for? The solo walk around the park? For what? In the earliest of days your tiny human doesn't give a fuck where you are, as long as there is milk, clean nappies and the perfect napping spot they really do not care. Whilst it might do you good to get out, it might not. If it is only going to add to the anxiety, stress and fear you have about being on show with a very unpredictable baby, then who are they to tell you it will do you good. Just do you and you will be the best version of yourself that you can possibly be in these early days.

My Fairy Godmothers!

Source – Disney Wiki –
As she herself explains, the Fairy Godmother is the embodiment of Cinderella's hope. She did not appear until Cinderella was at her weakest point.

I am more or less the last of those around me to have a baby. The guilt I feel for not being there for those before me is crushing. I was that childless friend, living her best life who would drop by every once in a while, and send the odd text to ask, how are you? How are you? This is the shittiest text you can send to someone who has just begun a journey into motherhood. Of all the things you are, even if you are smashing the shit out of motherhood, you are definitely not okay! I had not been there; I was oblivious to the overwhelming emotion and struggles that a new mama faces.

I was that friend who had no appreciation for those sleepless nights, just assuming that a new mama is tired and that is okay because it's part of the course. The lonely days, this was not even a consideration, they have a tiny baby why would they be lonely? Those moments of despair when you look at your tiny human and think, 'I don't know what I am doing, I cannot do this anymore.' These moments had been non-existent to me, I really had no idea.

Maybe now you can see the shock to my system when I had a baby, I really was that naive, that ignorant, that clueless. Whatever the word, that was I. I had no experience of any of this, I did not know that in those early days of motherhood my friend just wanted a hug, just wanted me to sit with them and acknowledge that this was shit and just wanted me to talk at them about anything other than the bloody baby.

So, to all those friends of mine who were mamas before me, I am sorry I wasn't there, I am sorry I didn't get it, I am sorry that I was absolutely useless. I just did not know. I will forever be there for those after me, now that I know just how much those around you matter in those times.

I was so lucky for the support I was surrounded by in my first weeks and months as a mama. I had an abundance of support, far greater than I ever expected and even then, I found this a desperate and lonely time. How women do this on their own with no support is beyond me, to me these mamas are true heroes. I don't know how you do it, all I do know is that you deserve a medal because it is the hardest thing in the world. I often used to think about those mamas doing it totally on their own. I remember thinking, how? How are you doing this? I was surrounded by support, support far greater than I ever expected to get and I was still finding this whole experience hell.

I will be forever grateful to my mum and mother-in-law; they truly were my fairy godmothers in those first few weeks. Those two angels I waited impatiently for in those first days, so happy to see their smiling faces walking through the front door.

My mother-in-law came every day in those first few weeks so that I could shower, have something to eat and to allow me to have an adult conversation. Well, kind of. She's pretty obsessed with her granddaughter so there was a lot of baby talk but she gave me enough to occupy my mind. You can't really do a conversation in these early days, you listen but you don't hear. All the same, it is so nice to just have someone talk at you. You are so grateful to have words being spoken at you instead of screams.

My mother-in-law would nurse my baby girl for the time she was there because unlike me, she had the ability to console her. I should have been sad about the fact that she could console my baby and I could not and sometimes I did feel sad about this, however for those hours of quiet, to watch my baby girl sleeping in her arms peacefully I would have given anything.

My mother-in-law would get me out of the house for a walk almost every day once we were past the first two weeks. She would also make me have something to eat. This is such a luxury in those first few weeks when you literally cannot find time to go the toilet! Once I was clean and fed, she would leave me to it and I would then anxiously count down the hours until my mum arrived.

My mum would arrive after work, usually after six-thirty p.m., she would help me to bathe the baby and settle her for bed. If the baby woke in the night, she would keep me company whilst I fed her before going back to sleep. She always had work the next day but she wanted to stay with us and wanted to offer her support for those late night feeds. In addition to holding down a job and trying to keep her daughter sane she was also supporting her mother with dementia. My mum is my hero, a real-life superwoman. If I can be half of what she is then I will be winning at life.

My mum, the woman who feared nothing had three children, two of which are twins. She had three children under-three so really, she must have been looking at the disaster her daughter had become, thinking come on lovely girl get a grip of your life. She, on occasion when I felt I could go on no more, gave me some tough motherly love. At the time I hated it, I really didn't want it, didn't need it, but in hindsight she was doing me a favour and looking back I laugh (out loud) at some of the things she said to me. They seemed so awful at the time in my sensitive state but really, they weren't that bad.

I clearly remember our first shopping trip to Tesco. Yet another nightmare and another shit thing to add to that ever-growing shit list I was working on. We walked through the door and the screaming began, I wanted to turn around and go home. My optimistic, fearless mother had a better idea, or so she thought. "Keep walking love, she will settle now." Now for some reason, maybe it's the anxiety, maybe it's the pain, or maybe it's the fact that you have absolutely no faith in your own decision-making anymore that you go along with this idea, go along with the optimism. The screaming is getting louder! "Give me the baby and the bottle, you go and do your shopping." Again, I listen and follow instruction, I don't know what I put in my trolley, but I am sure it was nothing I needed because all I wanted to do was get out of that supermarket. I ran around the aisles like a crazy woman, on reflection I most definitely was a crazy woman. I get back to my mother and baby girl, surprise, surprise she is still screaming. We drive home and she screams all the way.

By the time we get home my distress and upset has turned to that dreaded anger. I look at my mum in despair, my life is over, it is really over because I can't even go shopping and that is quite an essential basic task if you want to have food in your house. How am I ever going to get out of this bloody house? Why does she always scream, she is clean, fed, winded – what else does this tiny human need! And then those words of tough love come, "You need to get a grip, this is it, this is a baby, this is what they do!" Now that doesn't sound too bad, it isn't too bad but when your mum looks at you dead in the face and uses that mum tone, you know she means it. You know you have to get a grip and get on with this. There is no pity party here. No sympathy, no mollycoddling, just get a fucking grip, lovely girl.

Maybe, just maybe, this is what helped me pull through. My mum and my husband were both, I felt at the time harsh in their approach. I was struggling, really struggling, I was hurting, I was breaking but they were firm. I hated it at the time, it broke me more than I was already broken but what it meant was that I couldn't wallow in my self-pity. When the sympathy is removed you have to just get on with it. My response to feedback in any situation has always been; to firstly be hurt, quickly followed by a silent fuck you, now watch me do this and watch me do this good. That is not to sound horrible because honestly without them around me I couldn't have got to where I am now, but this is to say thank you, thank you for making me good at this, thank you for pushing me out of my darkest moments.

I really was and still am blessed with all of the support we have. I knew it at the time, and I know it now. Without the support of my fairy godmothers, I honestly don't think I would have made it through those weeks.

I would talk or moan to my fairy godmothers daily. Gosh, they must have really enjoyed coming to see me every day. I must have been such great company, such a joy to be around, so happy in my new role as mama - NOT!

For some reason they both had faith in me far greater than I did in myself. I remember thinking every day, they can't keep doing this, I have to learn to do this for myself although the thought of actually doing it myself and not seeing their faces every day frightened the living shits out of me.

Those two women were the only people on the planet who could console my baby, without them how the hell would we manage. For now, I could only long for the day my baby girl looked at me in the way she looked at my fairy godmothers.

Week six came, my mum was working and my mother-in-law was on holiday. This was it, my big moment! I was flying solo! And I was absolutely shitting myself.

I haven't mentioned yet, but my husband was working in London. His working week at the time would go like this; Monday leave at four a.m. and return Tuesday at ten p.m., Wednesday he would work from home, Thursday leave at four a.m. and return Friday at about six-thirty p.m. He was beyond exhausted! So we are heading into week six, we went to bed on the Sunday night, we were sleeping in separate rooms apart from on a Friday and Saturday night because my husband did not want to wake the baby at four a.m. or be woken by the baby before this on his limited sleep anyway. I lied in bed that Sunday night watching her sleeping in her next to me crib so peacefully, so perfect and I cried and cried and cried, I had that sickly back to school feeling in my belly. 'What am I going to do? What if she cries for the whole day?'

She woke at seven a.m., she was screaming. This was not an unusual start to the day; she was starving and screaming for her first bottle. My sickly belly had gone, I was still anxious as hell, but I knew I had to get up and get on with it, which is what I did.

Our day was not bad. Okay, so I was anxious, sweaty, shitting myself, didn't eat and definitely didn't sleep. But I did manage to have a shower, put my make up on and get dressed. I also walked to the doctors to register her. Not all bad. I can tell you this though, I had never been so happy to see my mum arrive at seven p.m. that night. To see an adult, have a conversation, to hear about her day and not just talk about a baby. It was pure heaven. It was how I used to feel about that first sip of wine you have on a Friday night after a shitty week in work. So, to summarise my mum's arrival had turned in to my Friday night wine.

And so, our week pretty much went like that until day four, she screamed non-stop and I mean non-stop. I couldn't put her down; she was on me all day, she didn't sleep she just screamed. I rang my mum in a fluster. "I'm going to run out of bottles, Mum." I literally couldn't even put her down to wash and sterilise her bottles. Now I was convinced there was something wrong with this baby. I mean I had thought this many a time in these first weeks, however generally at some point, on one of her bottles she would fall asleep, but not today.

My mum arrived at seven p.m., I had not showered, not ate, not even brushed my teeth. My poor baby girl was still screaming. I knew she was in pain, I could tell, I don't know how. Maybe that mother instinct had finally kicked in or something because I knew there was definitely something not right with her. We bathed her and still that did not provide any comfort to her, she was so distressed. After a long day she finally went to sleep at about eleven p.m. My mum, the woman who fears nothing, was concerned, I knew she was.

So, we wake, I have literally prayed all night long that whatever had bothered her be gone by the morning because and how stupid and selfish and pathetic is this! The thought of taking my poor screaming baby to the doctor's surgery and sitting in that waiting room was sending my anxiety through the roof. My prayers were not answered. It is a repeat of the previous day only worse. By one p.m. she is being so sick and is refusing her bottles. And so, the trip to the doctors.

I phone my mum to tell her I have to take her in to see the doctor, I end the call and she calls straight back, she wants to come with me. The relief! Now as much as I don't want her to leave work, I don't want to go to the surgery on my own even more.

I don't shower; don't brush my hair or my teeth - nothing. I throw on a pair of jeans and a top and we are gone. I am not joking when I say I was convinced she was seriously ill, in my mind this had to be a life-threatening illness.

The doctor took one look at my daughter and probably me in my sorry state, I am sure I must have actually smelt! He needed to call the paediatrician's for advice. He called us back in and said that they believed she had CMPA. Oh my God! What the fuck is CMPA?

It's okay, it is just a cow's milk protein allergy. Now I am not taking this lightly because it is awful, and some babies suffer extremely for years because of it but I would be lying if I said I wasn't relieved. I thought we were dealing with a life and death situation here based on how poorly and distressed she had been for these two days. By the time we arrived at the doctors her skin from head to toe was bright red and covered in a rash, put that together with the sickness, refusing bottles and non-stop screaming – you can kind of see how I got to a life-or-death situation in my panicked, sleep deprived mind, right?

After a prescription of new milk, a visit from the health visitor (the doctor had asked for her to visit me the next day, most likely after being presented with a broken mama in his office) and a further day of violent sickness to clear the final remnants of the cow's milk still lingering in her tummy she started to settle and so did I. It was far from even comfortable at this point, I was still a sweaty, anxious mess but the screaming did begin to ease as did my rapid beating heart.

So, to sum up the first week without my fairy godmothers

(in bullet points): -
- strong start
- slightly scary
- progressively worse
- horrendous
- an ever so distant pin prick of light starting to appear at the end of what seemed like an extremely long tunnel!

The main thing is we survived it and that was the best feeling in the world. Each week after the first, while my anxiety was still heightened, and I dreaded the crying and screaming, I started to find my feet just that little bit more.

When you are the only option, you get on with it. We were finally 'getting' each other. As the days and weeks went by, I found myself starting to understand her, what she wanted and when. I felt as though we were starting very slowly to communicate with one another. As much as I initially dreaded the time I would be alone with my baby it was what was needed for us.

There were still countless obstacles and many more public melt downs to suffer until we had completely worked one another out. But, as they say, the best is yet to come and in the first weeks of motherhood I couldn't agree with this statement more.

Mothercare Has the Best Baby-Feeding and Changing Rooms

Mothercare closing down is a crime! Based on my experience alone. I can only assume the decisionmaker on this had never used their facilities for an entire day whilst being a broken first-time parent.

How do I know this? Because between my mum and I, we spent six hours in the baby feeding room in Mothercare when my tiny human was around four weeks old. This is a true story, I kid you not.

I needed a few new mummy bits and bobs from Mothercare, mum persuaded me to go, dangling that positivity carrot once again that it would do us both good to get out of the house. When we arrived my daughter was sleeping. Great, I was starving! A quick pit stop in the cafe next door for a coffee and a bite to eat while she sleeps, this was our plan anyway.

Babies have this great ability to wake as soon as you are presented with a plate of food. Well, mine does anyway. And so, the screaming began, armed with a bottle and my mum, who, as I have previously mentioned is the woman who literally fears nothing, I was fine. 'I got this,' I thought, 'and if I haven't my mum will have.' We fed her and she kept screaming. We winded her and she kept screaming. We changed her and she kept screaming. We were stuck with this screaming tiny human in the café of a department store for what felt like forever. It is funny how that happens, when your tiny human has a meltdown, it is paralysing. In those early days instead of just getting up and leaving you feel trapped. You feel the need to soothe your baby before you can physically move.

This melt down was particularly bad, my anxiety was once again on the ceiling. I was sweating, profusely. I wanted the floor to open up. What happened next took me by complete surprise. A not so lovely woman who worked in said department store came across to us, she looked at me and my screaming baby and these words came out of her mouth: "My daughter is six and I've been thinking about having another baby but after hearing yours I've realised why I only have one and I don't want any more."

Yes, she actually said this! Now, I was not surprised by her opinion, as I said it was bad. I was surprised because she is the one before, she knows, she has been in my shoes. It is these kinds of comments that really boost your new mama confidence in these desperate situations – NOT! The pre-baby me would have told her where to take her horrible, shitty opinion. The post-baby, anxious, petrified of my tiny human me said nothing. Don't be this woman, us mama's need to stick together in this, if we don't have each other then we have nothing.

Anyway, she obviously hit a nerve because I wanted to get out of there as fast as I could. We foolishly thought that the short walk next door to Mothercare might settle her.

Unfortunately, it did not. We got to Mothercare and headed straight for the feeding/changing room to begin the changing, feeding, winding process again. For about the first twelve weeks my baby girl fed two- hourly during the day. This basically meant you spent the entire day feeding and winding her, by the time you had finished the process for bottle-one it was pretty much time to start again on bottle-two. So, we finish the process and she continues to scream. By now I am back on the ceiling, my nerves are wrecked, my body is aching where I am so tense with anxiety, fear and the dreaded anger. My mum tells me to go into the store and do my shopping, she will stay in the changing/feeding room with the baby.

Stupidly I try to do my shopping, I am so flustered I can't concentrate. I thoughtlessly throw anything into my basket, and I mean anything. Nothing I really came for or actually needed. I leave my basket and run back to check on the baby and my mum, she is still screaming, my mum is somehow and, in my opinion, weirdly, still calm. We swap places and mum pops into the store whilst I pathetically think I might be able to console my screaming baby. I already know I can't do this. I put her in the pushchair and take her for a walk outside, the fresh air might help to soothe her. A retail park seems so small when you walk the length and breadth of it five hundred times trying to settle your screaming baby who has absolutely no intention of settling.

I go back, I want to give up, but my mum is adamant that I finish my shopping and get what I came for. I am so defeated, I have not the energy to take on my fearless mother and explain to her that I can't do my shopping because I don't even remember what I came for in the first place. And guess what, it's already time for the next feeding process to begin. So off mum goes with my beautiful but very noisy baby girl to change her, feed her and wind her, again.

I am not joking when I say my mum actually made friends with people in those changing/feeding rooms. We will change their names to John and Joanne for the purpose of the book, but she actually showed me how John and Joanne (yes, she had got on first name terms with her new found friends) had taught her a new winding technique that we had not tried yet. I honestly believe people must have thought she was doing a demonstration of using the changing and feeding facilities in the store because she really did spend a whole day in that room.

I can't tell you that I learnt anything from this experience because I didn't, other than what great facilities Mothercare have. And that if I could do that day all over again, I would have left as soon as the screaming began. The problem is, that every time you have an experience like this it knocks any minute bit of confidence you have left and trust me there is not much left to lose. All it does is make the next outing even more daunting. But we do keep trying because we know we have to try our hardest to get back to having a life outside of those four walls that become so suffocating. The only saving grace I suppose was that we were in Mothercare, I am sure that a screaming baby for the poor staff who worked there was something they had to endure on a daily basis.

The screaming didn't end there though, the experience of visiting both a café and Mothercare was obviously very damaging for my poor baby girl because we got home that evening and the screaming continued. The hardest part of the continuous screaming other than the distress it causes to the both of you is that you do still have things to do. Even more so if you have spent a day out, you have to wash and sterilise the million bottles that you took with you. My question is, how do you do this when your tiny human is freaking out and you are alone?

You have two options:

Option One - you can put them down and leave them to scream. I tried this only a handful of times because really the wrenching pain in my heart and my stomach was too much. I know that it made no difference whether she was in my arms or alone at this point, however, to feel like you're neglecting your screaming baby on top of the inability to console them is unbearable.

Option Two - the sling, the wonderful baby sling that so many mamas rave about. I can attach my tiny human to me giving me two free hands to wash and sterilise bottles. DON'T try this alone when tiny human is already screaming! The screaming, that unbearable screaming got louder. After the worst day out, I am in a right pickle, tiny human is stuck to me in a sling, my fluster has disabled me entirely, I cannot fathom this stupid piece of material out to release her! My baby girl is screaming at full pelt now, we are both sweating because the skin-to-skin contact is emphasised by the fact that we are tied together and hysteria kicks in. With tears once again rolling down my cheeks I become hysterical, I cannot stop laughing. How pathetic has my life become, I am now in my living room with tiny human, sorry let me rephrase – with screaming tiny human attached to me, stuck to me with no way of releasing her. Blinded by overwhelming levels of fear and anxiety my brain has chosen this moment to finally give up on me. I mean, if anyone were to see the sorry state of me in that moment, I think I would be writing this in Broadmoor.

I called my mum, she came back, she released us, and she stayed the night. In those moments as I looked to my mama, my fairy godmother, my fearless, powerful mother I wished my baby girl would in time look at me the way I look at her. I also wished that I could have an ounce of that fearlessness that she had rocked for the majority of my lifetime.

The Public Meltdown of all Meltdowns!

A public melt down not to be confused with an episode of newborn crying. A public meltdown includes, but is not limited to, newborn screaming continuously for more than ten minutes, refusal of bottle, refusal of dummy and the heightened noise of that scream when random stranger member of the public tries to pull a funny face at tiny human.

I was on maternity leave at the same time as two of my work colleagues. That shared interest our tiny humans, brought us together. It is nice to spend time with those you know regardless of how close your friendship was before baby, especially in those early days.

That is not to discredit my new mama friends because I have grown super close to many of them and hold a genuine love for all of them. I have found that, that 'love' develops naturally, you realise you wouldn't have become friends if it wasn't for your tiny human, but you know you are in this together. You are all trying to make this an enjoyable experience even on the most shittiest of days when your tiny human has awoken as a monster. On these days no matter what you do for them they hate you! It is those days that these mama friends are the most important, you look them dead in the eye whilst you are red in the face, full of tears and ready to have a meltdown yourself and they don't need to say a thing. The look of understanding is enough to see you through your shitty day.

Anyway, I digress, back to my work friends. We decide to go for a walk around Roath Park, that's a safe outing. I go there all the time so what would be daunting about this outing for me, this is a normal day out for my daughter and I. We meet at one p.m. and walk around the lake, it is very relaxed, and my daughter falls asleep, perfect. We go into the café and whilst she is asleep I grab the opportunity to run to the counter and choose my food. I go for a sandwich because if she wakes, it won't go cold, and I only need one hand to eat keeping the other free to nurse my baby girl if I need to, can I? Do I really have that ability? Do I hell! I would say the mistake I had made here was in thinking that this outing would be successful. I was obviously too cock-sure and getting too big for my new mama boots to believe this was going to be an enjoyable experience. Was I that stupid to have so quickly forgotten that my baby girl hated public spaces and people?

I come back to the table and my friend is nursing my daughter, she is screaming. Oh God, stay calm mama, stay calm. It's okay, I have a bottle at the ready, I am prepared for this. I give her the bottle but she doesn't want it. This is new to me, despite everything, the screaming, the meltdowns she always wanted her bottles. It must be her nappy, I take her to the changing room. The whole time she is screaming, full force, top of the lungs screaming. I know it's bad because people are looking at me horrified. This café is normally full of mothers and babies, a safe space, today however, typically we are the only mothers and babies in the café.

I come back from changing her and try the bottle again, she is having none of it. My food arrives and I am far too distressed to attempt to eat it with my screaming tiny human in my arms.

For twenty minutes I try everything I can to console her. People are looking on in horror, some people are coming over and trying to talk to her, this only making her worse. My tiny human does not like other humans, please people help this desperate mama out right now and fuck off. I look at my friends with tears in my eyes, I have nothing left, literally nothing. "I'm going to take her home," I say, they nod and smile, that is all I need, and I am out of there.

I get home and she is full of smiles. I can't believe it. I want to be mad at her but how can I be with that smile. I laugh but it hurt me, it hurt me bad that I was still unable to console my baby. I thought we had this by now, I thought we were over the public meltdowns. My confidence was absolutely hammered. I didn't want to go out EVER again.

I came home and searched every online forum I could, demanding an answer to why my daughter hated public places and people. Now if you haven't yet used one of these online forums, I urge you to not use it as your go to tool when you are still sweating from your dilemma. If you are lucky, you will get a reply from one or two mamas just like you or I but be prepared for the replies from the righteous, perfect mamas who have never had a bad day in their life. They have no perspective of reality! So my replies came in;

- **give her time** – Thirteen weeks I've given to this, how much time does she need!
- **everything is new to her, imagine yourself in her shoes** – Imagine yourself in my shoes, bitch!
- **keep trying, don't give up** – um really? You think this is worth pursuing?
- **go somewhere quieter!** - A fucking walk without company is quiet, my house is quiet, my car is quiet!

I wanted to smash my phone up! None of these answers offered me a glimmer of hope or support in my desperation. I know people meant well but I wanted someone to give me a magic remedy to make our outings easier, enjoyable, manageable I would have settled for. All those replies did was piss me off and made me feel once again like a piece of shit who had a baby she could not console. It was fine for those righteous mothers to offer advice, they had never had a public melt down, they didn't understand my desperation. Well, that is how I felt about them and their shit advice anyway.

You may think that their advice was nice, kind, and supportive but in that moment, I wanted support for me. I didn't want people to think about my tiny human, I wanted people to think of me. I wanted them to realise how difficult I was finding this. I wanted them to say, I had the same problem, and this is what I did.

The problem mamas is this: if you speak to anyone who has had a baby more than two years ago, they have by now actually forgotten how bloody hard it is. If you speak to someone who has had the 'perfect' baby, they don't, wont and can't understand how you are feeling. How could they? They have never experienced a public melt down where you literally want the floor to swallow you whole. Talking to these people offers you no help or support, and so, I have found in my months of research and these online forums that it is always those mamas who reply. The ones who have all but forgotten what it's like, the ones who have never been phased by a meltdown, or worse still the ones who have never experienced a meltdown.

You need to talk to mamas who are going through this now. You need to find those mamas who haven't been tricked by their tiny human three years on, who look at them and remember every day of their life so far being peachy. You both want and need someone to say to you it is shit, it is totally shit but it will get better.

I wanted an exact time of when this would get easier. I was literally ready to give up and lock us both away for the rest of my maternity leave, once again! I had paid to start a 'Baby Development Class' the following week. I had one week to decide if I would keep us safe from any future public humiliation by locking us away forever or if I would brave it one last time and have a final attempt at getting us both out.

I chose the latter, maybe that part of the person who I was, the old me, the pre-mama me was making an appearance. This decision following the nightmare I had just lived in that café in Roath Park seemed ridiculous, but I think of all my decisions in those early days this was by far the best.

Back to the Roath Park incident, I was still not over it when my husband came home from work that evening. I shared with him my awful experience. By now, he thought his wife, the woman he had married just three years ago, had been taken away by aliens and replaced by a crazy woman. He was sick to death of my moaning! What I failed to see at that point in our lives is that by not communicating my feelings to my husband he didn't know that I was struggling every minute of every day. In his eyes I had exactly what I had longed for, for so long. I was spending every minute of every day with our daughter, and whilst I envied him going to work and resuming so much of his 'normal life', work, lunch, conversation, hot coffee, a pint with colleagues after work he envied the time I was having with our daughter. The time he was sacrificing to provide for us.
In my heightened anxiety and fear stricken state I had missed that. I was blinded to the reality that he was struggling also but

whilst I had ample opportunity to work on building the bond between my daughter and I, he did not. He had to try and slot in to our lives every time he returned from work, he had no daily opportunity to learn the new us. To him in that moment, I believe he felt that he had lost his wife, lost his sleep and had limited time to spend with his daughter whilst carrying the load of providing for his family in a very stressful job.

I was able to see that much later on but at the time it passed me by. This meant we spent far too many months not only on different pages but in different books.

I felt a lot of jealousy at the time, jealous that he was able to get away from this and I was not. I also felt very lonely, he had always been my rock and whilst I hadn't shared with him my deep dark truths I thought he knew. I thought that whilst I was trying my best to hide this from the rest of the world it was obvious to those closest to me. I think in truth I probably wanted them to know. I know now that I was doing a good job of hiding my true feelings because everyone around me had no idea until they read this book.

My husband had always been my rock, he had always been there, cheering me on, pulling me up and pushing me forward. I wanted a hug, I wanted him, someone, anyone to tell me that this was going to get better. The problem was that he was away from his baby girl for most of the week and therefore his level of understanding was diminishing. I can appreciate this now, but I couldn't at the time. In that mindset this had two effects on me;

One – It pissed me off and made me even more insular because really if I couldn't talk my darkest truths to him then who could I share them with.

Two – It spurred me on to get good at this, to get out of the house and enjoy my time with my precious baby girl. So, I proceeded with my best efforts to get bloody good at this, to be the mama that I imagined I would be and that I so desperately wanted to be.

I decided not to give up, not to lock us away from the world but to nail this whole motherhood thing in the outside world. To get past these meltdowns, to start enjoying the two of us outside in the real world. Even if it scared the shit out of me, being trapped inside forever becoming a lonely, isolated mess scared me even more. I had to dig deep, pull up my big girl pants and start to nail the shit out of this motherhood thing. For my own sanity!

Baby Classes

Where I found myself, well not my whole self but my new self. Where I could see other new mamas in a safe space – see meltdowns from other babies apart from mine. Where I didn't make lifelong friends but where I found friends for that moment. Friends who kept me sane for that moment.

So, I braved it!

The week after the Roath Park melt down, we were both up, dressed and ready for our first Baby Development Class. I was dreading it! I spent the night before and the morning of talking myself into it. I was so tempted to give in, to not go.

I didn't care about the money I spent. The thought of my baby kicking off in this class and not being able to console her in a room full of 'perfect' mamas with 'perfect' babies, because of course in my mind that's how it was going to be, was frightening the life out of me. I had to do it. I knew if I didn't go that would be it, I wouldn't go anywhere ever again. I'm exaggerating, slightly but I would have locked myself away until she was at least old enough to talk to me and therefore tell me what it is that she wants because so far this mother's instinct thing for me was non-existent. I never seemed to know what the bloody hell she wanted.

Just in time for said baby class we were 'between cars', of course we were! Therefore, we would travel to our first baby class by taxi. I mean talk about a giant step for mama and tiny human, not only did I have to endure this baby class I had to get us both in a fucking taxi first. By now, I know she hates the car, so this was really enticing me to attend this class, NOT.

The taxi arrived, I load in baby, pushchair and changing bag and we make our way. My tiny human screams all the way there, great start. Just as the taxi pulls up to the venue, she falls asleep. Fucking great, she finally sleeps, and I am going to have to wake her up for this baby class. Now, there is no expectation to wake a sleeping baby for this baby class BUT after all of the effort to just get us here there is no way I could let her sleep this one out.

A big, long deep breath and we're in. She wakes instantly! The class teacher bounces over to us, huge smiles, loud, in her face. My stomach fell out of my arse. My daughter hates people and now this stranger is in her face. Bad start, the worst start, more horrific than I could have anticipated, she is going to scream the place down! But guess what, she didn't, she smiled.

Oh my God, now this woman must be the baby whisperer. How the hell did she do that? I was gob smacked. Okay, good start, very good start. I can feel that tiny bit of confidence making its reappearance. I make my way to the mats. If you haven't been to a baby class yet you will become familiar with the mats. Basically, all mamas sit in a 'U' shape on said mats facing the teacher with your tiny human led in front of you. My heart is in my mouth. I peer around this 'U' that I find myself sat in, eyeing up the other mamas and their babies. I don't know what I am expecting to see but I am trying to take it all in, I am trying to secure that smile I have painted on my face and trying to count my breaths and remain calm. Calm mama, calm baba – allegedly.

And so, it begins with the dreaded introductions. You have to give your name, your baby's name, how old your baby is and one good thing that has happened this week. Okay, breathe.

I now have to take my heart out of my mouth so that I can speak and remember those few basic facts – my name, my baby's name and how old she is. That should be easy enough. I also have the tricky task of trying to think of one good thing that has happened this week. This is tricky because, I realise in that moment that until this point, I had never appreciated anything about our days. There hadn't been any good moments as far as I was aware. I was so conscious that I was missing any good moments, to this point they had been masked by the unimaginable fear.

I went for honesty, I told the class that my baby hates public places and new people and therefore if we made it through this class without a meltdown then this would be our good thing from this week. The teacher was lovely, she smiled and said, "Do what you need to do today, if you need to go to the back of the room or outside to console your baby then you do it. Do whatever you need to do for you and your baby, forget about us." And breathe. We had made it through the introductions and probably the first ten minutes of the class, only thirty minutes to go. Come on, we can do this!

I was slowly starting to relax, we were ten minutes in, and my daughter hadn't had a meltdown. In fact, she seemed to be enjoying herself. She was having a nose around the room, she was smiling at all of the other babies. Then the unexpected happened, another baby had a meltdown, and then another. It was the first time in fourteen weeks that I had seen other babies have meltdowns. Melt downs just like my baby. The difference between me and those other mamas was that they were not phased by their babies' meltdowns, in fact, nobody was phased by those meltdowns. I was in a safe space and even more than that, I realised for the first time in fourteen weeks that this was 'normal'. This was what all babies did, not just mine. I was so happy, elated in fact. That's quite sick I suppose, to be happy about other mamas having to deal with the meltdowns that I so dreaded but selfishly I was over the moon. In my defence, they didn't seem to be flustered like me, I'm sure I would not have taken so much joy in this if they had been. Just like that, my fear left. Such a release, such a shift, everything felt different in that moment.

The isolation I had been subjecting myself to, meant I hadn't understood that what I was going through was normal. That babies do have meltdowns and they are not always easily consoled, it wasn't just us. This was it.

She did have a little cry in the class but just because she was hungry, I gave her a bottle and winded her and she was fine. No screaming, no melt down, just smiles. Wow! I had read and been told so many times that like an animal a baby can smell your fear and will feed from that. I hadn't believed this, I couldn't believe this because I could not until this point release that fear. I could see then, in that moment that my anxiety had been transferring to my baby. I am no scientist or doctor, do not claim to be and do not want to be but I can only assume that this is what had been happening.

I got home and I felt like superwoman. I was so happy, we both were! I messaged my husband, my mum, my mother-in-law, those around me who had been desperate for me to shake a leg and that bloody fear at the same time. Charged up with a new lease of mama confidence I decided that if this was the way my baby girl was comfortable out of the house then I must immediately find another baby class to take her to. We found Monkey Music, I signed up that same day for the following week.

I was nervous, really nervous on our way to Monkey Music.

What if the previous week had been a fluke? Heart in my mouth, nerves at the forefront we went along. Deep breath and in we go.

A smiling face. "HI, lovely," said another mama, a 'normal' mama that friendly face and welcoming from a stranger was just what I needed. I could breathe again. The nice thing about meeting other mamas is that you never get stuck for conversation, you both share common ground in your tiny human, and you are both pleased to see an adult. We chatted with ease, I told her of my tiny humans 'problems' with public places and people. It was so nice. It was so nice to talk to another adult, especially in that moment of heightened anxiety, waiting for that class to begin, hoping that she enjoyed it, praying that she didn't have a meltdown.

The door opens, another smiling face, the teacher welcoming us into the room. The class begins, this one is loud. Instruments, lot of instruments. I am tense, she doesn't like noise! The clue was in the bloody name, what was I expecting. This could have been a huge mistake on my part, but that's okay it would just be yet another thing to add to the ever- growing shit list. She surprised me again, she seemed to really enjoy it and she loved the noises and the other babies. Again, like in the baby class she had a little cry but I fed her, winded her and she was fine. No melt down! PROGRESS! Superwoman is actually here, I felt amazing.

And so, we continued with these two classes every week and we loved them. I made some really good friends. My daughter very rarely had a cry and if she did it was very easy to console her, a little cuddle, distraction or a bit of reassurance and she was fine.

I would encourage any new mama to try a baby class. If you are at that point of wanting to lock yourself away and give up on the idea of entering any public place with your tiny human ever again for the sake of your remaining sanity, then I would say it is the perfect time for you to try one. It was the first time I had realised that all babies cry. It was the first time that I realised there are mamas all over the place going through what you are going through.

Feeling the same way that you are feeling only they are laughing about it. Laughing within that safe community that they have found for themselves. I also learnt a few tips from other mamas by watching how they dealt with their babies' meltdowns. The most important one being to remain calm!

The thing about these classes is that their sole purpose is to serve mama (or dada) and baby. You are not going to present them with anything they haven't seen today, yesterday, the day before and tomorrow. Really, you are not unique in this journey, even though you may feel as though you are. You are in a safe space, nobody bats an eye. Feeding and changing is no big deal. It doesn't matter if you arrive a few minutes late because the class is full of mamas and babies so the chances are you will not be the only late arrival and if you are everyone understands. It really did do wonders for both my daughter and I.

In fact, my daughter transformed within weeks of those classes to the one in the class who loved every bit of attention she could get – oh and she worked for it. She quickly became the class clown, known as 'smiler' and then later 'chatterbox' by all her teachers and the mamas in our groups. She loves to be the centre of attention and demands it with a big, massive strop if it is not all about her. She would put her arms out to strangers for a cuddle, before the stranger danger phase came. Though when she realised stranger danger meant less attention that phase passed by so quickly. Talk about a dramatic turn around. Age, confidence, classes, calm mama - whatever the answer, I do not know for sure, but I do know that it all coincided with these baby classes. I truly believe that there has to be something in them. It cannot be that much of a fluke, I won't believe it.

These classes are one of the many things I missed the most when I went back to work. Especially as she got older and thrived on interaction with other children. I tried to keep the classes going but the week became too hectic, and it just couldn't work for us. They are the place you go for an hour a day where you literally focus your full attention to your child. No distraction of housework or chores, just to enjoy being in the moment with your baby.

Jess

To the woman who probably doesn't know just how much of a massive dose of medicine she was to me in my darkest of days.

Meeting a new mama friend is what I can only imagine is a similar experience to that of online dating. You talk for a few weeks on one of the many mummy apps you have downloaded and then you arrange the first meet, the first date! The only difference to an actual date is that, well, other than the fact that you probably don't fancy them, (maybe you do but that's for another book!) is that when you arrive joining you is your tiny human. Now, if your tiny human is a screamer like mine was, this means that the first conversation that goes with a date, which should be exciting and interesting, is strained and difficult whilst you both try your best to 'talk' over the screaming baby. It is this difficulty that does not offer you the same comfort that you have from meeting people you already know. In addition to this, you also have the dreaded fear that the new mama you are meeting will have one of those 'perfect babies' who doesn't scream, worse still doesn't even cry. If this is the case then what the fuck will you; a crazy, flustered mama look like while you try and maintain composure. Trying your best to appear calm on the surface whilst all the while flapping like a panicked duck trying to provide a decent conversation.

This was how I met Jess, who came to be one of my best friends. Who I talk with almost every single day.

The first day I met Jess I took my beautiful cousin with me who herself had just become a first-time parent. She was one of us now. My tiny human was the eldest of the three babies and so whilst Jess and my cousin chatted it away for the hour or two we spent together I spent the entire time negotiating with my tiny human who was by now, far more active and alert which meant no chatter time for this mama. Nevertheless, Jess was not put off by this and we arranged to meet the following week in Roath Park.

I was nervous, it was just the two of us going this time. The familiar face of my cousin would not be there. What if I could not hold a conversation? I mean, whilst I was getting to grips with this whole motherhood thing and had just started to feel like I was doing kind of a good job, by this point I had nothing to talk about other than my tiny human. This is normally fine in a mummy meet up situation but as the months were going by, I was growing more and more conscious of the fact that I was losing my identity. I was a mother. I had nothing else to offer.

I had got better by now though at sticking to plans, I didn't cancel. She was like a breath of fresh air, the first words she uttered to me was that her tiny human was being an absolute diva. I loved her, she was honest. I relaxed. We spent about five hours together, we must have got some serious steps in because we walked laps and laps of the lake and the flower gardens of Roath Park. We stopped for a coffee and to feed our babies but aside from that we walked and talked. She talked about everything other than babies! She told me about her wedding that was to be the following year, her family, her work. I loved her.

She made me realise that all of things about you from before still exist. Maybe they are on hold for just now, but they are still a massive part of you, they are you and so for that reason they are still relevant. Even though you are on maternity leave you do still have a job to talk about. Even though your family are totally besotted with your tiny human and have nothing much else to talk to you about there is lots to tell about them. Your husband is still your husband, even though you are both slight strangers to one another these days whilst this tiny human dictates when you talk to each other, when you share a bed, when you kiss or hug. I found it so good to talk about my husband. About how we met, how long we had been together, about us. These parts of my life, important parts of my life had felt so distant.

We met every week for the rest of my maternity leave, sometimes two or three times a week. She saved me in many ways and I don't even think she realises it. She is so happy, so positive and so hilariously funny.

To me she was owning the shit out of motherhood, she wasn't phased by it, that was the impression she gave. What she showed me was that even though this tiny, demanding person had rocked up in your life and taken what felt like the whole of you that was just untrue. Whilst it is undeniably true that they do take a whole lot of you, you can still be you. You can still focus on things outside of this tiny human. Jess gave me other things to talk about, to my husband, my friends, my mum. Whilst I had spent the last however many months feeling as though I had completely lost myself Jess was interested in me. She asked about me, about my family, my work, my friends. I hadn't disappeared behind my tiny human when I was with her. I might have thought I had completely disappeared but that was my problem because I was still right there. All of the things that had made me 'me', were still right there and she helped me to see that. I had decided to close the whole box of me whilst I put every focus into my tiny human.

Whilst Jess was clearly besotted with her beautiful, gorgeous tiny human and her days and plans revolved around her, she had not forgotten herself and all of the wonderful things that were important to her. She talked about things other than babies, I had lost this ability the moment my tiny human arrived and took over my life with that all-consuming fear. It was not out of choice that I felt this my only conversation topic but those surrounding me talked to me about nothing other than my tiny human and therefore I felt irrelevant. Not in a pity party, woe is me kind of way but in a, this is what it is about now, this is what it is all about now.

Jess gave me that 'girly' chat topic back that I had missed so much!

For me she was my little bit of medicine that I took at least once a week. I learnt so much from her. I found much more of me again, not the whole me, but she made me feel important, she made me feel like I had far more purpose than being a mama, she made me realise and remember that I was a person before my tiny human and that that person still existed.

She will always hold a massive place in my heart. She will always be my breath of fresh air. She will always be one of my best friends.

Thank you Jess, from the bottom of my heart. For lots more than you know.

Food, Glorious Food!

In my time as a mama so far, I have learnt that many of the things I imagined I would love and find exciting turned out the be the ones I disliked the most or particularly struggled with. I once read that our memories over time become imagination. We only remember the best bits of situations that once were and in turn we imagine the rest subconsciously. To me, motherhood is just that but in flip reverse. Imagination and fantasy are often far better than the reality, though in turn the memories of those hellish first days quickly become imagination. When you relive them in your mind as the happiest most content moments of your life.

Yuck! This was probably my least favourite part. The never-ending weaning journey, full of excitement and discovery apparently. I hated it. I had a choker. My phobia when I started on this weaning journey, passed onto me by my husband, was choking and I was blessed with a bloody choker. It didn't begin this way, but I will share with you my story so you can understand my 'distaste' for this.

Feeding two-hourly was a chore, a pain in the arse if we are brutally honest about it! It would take my tiny human an hour to drink a bottle followed by half an hour of screaming whilst we frantically turned her into every position possible to try and wind her. By the time this was done it was time to start the next feed. My poor baby girl suffered horrendously with wind or colic or whatever the hell it was, it was so bad that I used to dread feeding her because of the screams of pain and discomfort that would follow. Considering that I would spend the majority of my days feeding her then this was a dread that remained a constant throughout most of the day.

I longed for the day when I was able to give her food. When I could feed her without causing her so much pain and distress. When I could get out of the house without needing to give her a bottle as soon as I arrived at wherever it was, we were heading. Then worrying whilst feeding her that a public meltdown would follow. It was a vicious cycle, despite discussing it with the health visitor every time we seen her there was nothing we could do for her other than what we were doing because it wasn't reflux. Gripe water and infacol were suggested over and over again, these did nothing for her. If anything, I think they actually made her worse.

Twelve weeks is when this will pass, I was told by everyone. I went to see the health visitor when she was eighteen weeks old about this bloody wind or colic or whatever it was, it wasn't easing. In fact, it seemed to be getting worse. I couldn't bear seeing her in so much pain after every feed. It seemed cruel, it felt as though I was causing the distress to her every time I gave her a bottle. The truth was, we didn't know what it was because this poor tiny human could not tell us, but the screaming would suggest she was in pain. Those magic words were spoken, "Try introducing some food." I was so happy!

I waited until the weekend to offer her the 'good' stuff so that my husband was able to take part in this milestone. In the meantime, I offered her baby rice as suggested by the health visitor. She tasted it and looked at me in disgust. If she could speak, I imagined she would say, "Yuck! What the fuck is this that you put into my mouth? Why would you feed me this awful tasting shit? Give me my delicious, warm, sweet tasting milk, you absolute monster." This was not the reaction I was expecting. I was deflated. Appreciating that this was a whole new experience to tiny human I persevered.

In that first week it went from bad to worse, by the end of the week she was point blank refusing to open her mouth. That jaw was remaining firmly locked for the foreseeable, the only thing passing her lips was a bottle and she was quite certain on that. I do admire the strength, determination and will of a tiny human. Although sometimes it is downright frustrating it is what most of us wish we had in all aspects of our life. To be that sure of ourselves, to be that determined, that decisive. At what point does this get lost for the many of us? When do we begin to compromise even when we disagree wholeheartedly? When do we begin to doubt our own self? I don't know the answer to that, what I do know is that my tiny human is my very own Beyonce, she is the strongest little lady I know. The distraction tactic, she uses that on me, and this is the level of genius I am blessed with.

Back to the weaning! What I have since learnt is that baby rice offers no taste and no nutritional value, so mama if this is not for your tiny human skip this step. I'm not really sure why baby rice is so highly promoted as the first step. Would you appreciate being offered bland, nothing food? No! Go straight to porridge instead.

Following the first week with no success I of course turned to my trusted Dr Google. The advice given at this point was:
- ❖ Let your baby take the lead
- ❖ Don't make food time become a chore and something that becomes a bad experience for your baby.
- ❖ Take it slow.

❖ Offer the spoon but don't force your baby to take it.

So, we took a few days off and went back to our usual bottle routine.

After the disapproval of the baby rice from my tiny human the following week we tried introducing some fruit. Now, offering fruit before veg is definitely frowned upon, always do veggies first is the advice. Whatever! I was eager for my baby girl to like food and therefore I didn't care what we did first, all that mattered to me was that she started to experience food. Veg first – what a stupid rule. Or so I thought. Apples were first and she loved them. Couldn't get enough. We couldn't get the spoon to her mouth quick enough. RESULT!

So, after the apple success I thought I better try my tiny human with some veggies, and this, fellow mamas is why you try veg first. It seems so obvious now, but this passed me by at the time. Fruit is deliciously sweet for your tiny human, thus only leading to sheer disappointment when you introduce 'boring' veg. Don't get me wrong, I'm not slagging off veg here, I love veg but if someone gave me a choice of peas or apples for the next three days, I'm going to take the apples. Carrots were up first, and she was furious about it. Again she presented me with that face, that face that was saying, "Why are you doing this mama, we have been over this already. Now stupid human give me back that lovely, sweet spoonful of delicious tasting apples please." Oh, dear God I panicked, how would I explain this to the health visitor?

Why do we do this? Why do we feel so pressurised to take the health visitor's word as absolute? Okay, appreciate that they are there to offer support, advice and 'best practice' but really that tiny human is yours. You are ultimately responsible to make all decisions for this person who belongs to you for the next eighteen years, at least. Where will the health visitor be when you are having a meltdown because your sixteen-year-old has gone to a house party and is totally pissed? Nowhere, mama, that's where they will be, bloody nowhere! So just relax, mama, there is no grown woman or man that I know who is still being spoon-fed pureed apples for breakfast, dinner and tea because that is what their mama introduced to their pallet first.

The failing in the weaning journey once again was mine. I had put too much unrealistic expectation on how this weaning journey would go. I had naively, perhaps stupidly, assumed that by the end of the month we would be on three meals a day inclusive of all nutrients and goodness that my tiny human needed. Of course, this is not the case, how silly was I to think this. Our tiny humans love their milk, it is all they have known. That delicious warm milk; the closeness of that cuddle you give them whilst you are feeding them, the familiar taste and that disgusting smell that they seem to love. Why on earth would they want to give this up for this weird tasting, weird textured object you would put into their mouth?

The weaning journey was a long one for us, after two weeks of point-blank refusing to open her mouth I gave up on the food for a week to give her a break (and my anxiety). I didn't want food to become a 'bad' thing for her. So far, all I had learnt was that she loved apples and hated carrots. After a week off we tried again, this time starting with veg, again she still wasn't keen, she would take maybe two spoonful's and then again lock that mouth shut. Trust me, despite numerous attempts and our best efforts of trying to lure her into opening her mouth she was not to be fooled. These tiny humans are very cute! They know what we are doing. "Do you think I'm stupid, woman? Put down that spoon and give me the goddamn bottle."

Persevere, mama! I've learnt as a mama you have to do a lot of persevering with your tiny human. Well with mine I do anyway, she is already a strong, independent woman and there is nothing that girl will do unless she wants to. Everything is very much on her terms. I do love and admire this about her, although frustrating at times.

I had very much had this idealistic view of baby led weaning. Chopping her food into finger sized portions whilst we ate alongside one another. This was a disaster! She choked on everything. I once again turned to my health visitor for advice, some babies take longer to get to grips with this than others. Persevere (there that word is again – I have a feeling I will be persevering for the rest of my life), stick to mashed food but keep trying.

At around six months she was slowly beginning to enjoy her new experience with food. I had to this point relied on Ella's Kitchen pouches. No, they are not cheap but they are super convenient. I kept this deep dark secret to myself when talking to my mama friends. Why would I confess to not cooking for my baby girl? They would spend hours of their week preparing meals from scratch for their babies. The truth is, I was nervous, I was paranoid that I would poison her. Based on my early motherhood experiences my rule was that if something caused me stress or anxiety, I simply would not do it.

My deep dark secret of Ella's Kitchen pouches started to bother me. I should cook for her, this is not right. What kind of a mama am I if I can't cook for my baby girl? So, when she was around seven months old I braced myself, I took the plunge! We went to the supermarket, and I did a food shop for my tiny human. I came home and started cooking up a storm of sweet potatoes, peppers, carrots, and broccoli. Anything healthy, nutritious and recommended for baby's first foods I had bought it. I would mix and blend them and then sit her in the highchair for her to eat mamas delicious cooking. I felt like a proper mama! Two spoonful's and she gave me that look. For fuck sake! I tried this for a week and for that whole week she would give me 'that look'. Needless to say, we reverted back to the Ella's Kitchen pouches, this time I was guilt free. Just as she had refused my boob in those early days, she was now refusing my cooking. The cost and waste of preparing her meals myself had cost me more than the bloody pouches.

Do what works for you mama. If you love to spend time in the kitchen preparing meals for your tiny human and if you are a freezer/re-use pro, then knock yourself out. For me it just wasn't worth the time, effort and cost and also slightly damaging for my ego when my baby girl looked at me in utter disgust over what I was serving her. She loved the pouches, and they were so handy when we were out and about, they are full of organic goodness and they were a godsend on our first holiday.

So down to two meals a day, snacks and three bottles I thought we had nailed this weaning journey and we were making strong progress. However, unbeknown to me she was going to throw a curve ball and refuse to be fed. Shit storm looming!

At eight months old my little 'Beyonce' had found a new level of independence, she wanted to feed herself. She woke up one morning and decided that being spoon fed by her mama was far too babyish. Now apparently, this is a milestone achievement. This is a good sign. The only one slight problem being that my tiny human chokes on everything unless it is mashed.

So, my question is this, how the fuck do you allow your tiny human to feed themselves porridge or any food of mashed substance when they cannot or will not use a spoon? I tried to be one of those free-spirited mamas and let her use her hands but oh my goodness the mess. I probably could have lived with the mess of this situation if she actually had a belly full of food by the time the chaos of mealtime was over. The food ended up all over her, all over the floor basically anywhere but her mouth!

Perhaps it was the food? Time to revert back to mamas cooking. Slightly less anxious now that we had made progress I downloaded 'Annabel Karmels' app. Mama these recipes are delicious and come with easy-to-follow instructions. I chose a few meal options that I thought my tiny human would like that also took care of the cow's milk allergy, I bought the ingredients and I was ready to go.

Week one – I thought I could cook each meal daily just before her dinner time. What a stupid idea. I mean my tiny human has not a clue in this world what 'patience' means, she is also lacking the enjoyment of her own company. So the prep and cooking time was very distressing for her and my fingers as I tried to chop like Gordon Ramsey without his many culinary skills! A positive from week one, she absolutely loved the food. She devoured every meal and happily let me feed her. So this was definitely a success but I needed to rethink the cooking part, she was not happy for this to be done on her time.

Week two – My solution to the week one problem was to prepare the meals the night before. So once tiny human was tucked nicely in bed, I would have my dinner and then begin preparations to cook her meals for the next day. What this actually meant was that I was 'finishing' my day and sitting down for some time to myself around eleven p.m. each night. This was a nightmare and not the right solution. When my husband got home on Thursday night I was exhausted! There has to be a better way.

Week three – Batch cook all of her meals on the weekend for the following week. So I started to cook at eight p.m. on Saturday night and finished cooking at one a.m. This was not ideal, definitely not ideal but at least I would have a few evenings back to myself.

It was going well, she was loving the meals however the hours of cooking was taking its toll.

I was knackered. My husband went shopping the following weekend, he came home with some Cow and Gate jars (as well as every brand of baby food jars that he could find – to beg an plead with me to stop cooking all night every night and have a rest). Please try these he said, he was worried I was doing too much. She loved them. From that point we opted for a combination of home cooking and jars.

When I was with one of my new mama friends recently she mentioned that she was attending a weaning course. I nearly spat my coffee in her face. A fucking weaning course! Are you joking? Why didn't I know about this bloody weaning course? Thanks for that information absolutely NO ONE! If I had known this at the time, I definitely would have booked onto one. I once again had no clue at what I was supposed to be doing here and I was shitting myself about it. I approached our weaning journey as I approached my journey into motherhood. I was winging it, badly mostly!

I am sure these weaning courses didn't exist when we were kids as my mother would say and we all seem to be able to eat without difficulty so I don't think it's the end of the world. However, if like me you're unsure, nervous and want some advice and reassurance then I would encourage you to find your local course and book onto it. Given our weaning experience I am sure it would have been extremely beneficial to us.

Throughout our weaning journey we learnt that our tiny human LOVES food and there is no way that girl goes hungry. She eats more than me, I honestly don't know how she does it, it is impressive.

Although I found this a difficult journey, one that I expected to enjoy and did not, as she got to around nine months old when she could feed herself and handled most foods well it became a pleasure to watch her eat. When we would eat out we would order her a children's meal or something tailored to what she likes and we would have so much enjoyment and fun. It is crazy to think it only took nine months for us to get back this part of our 'life'. Although going out for food now is very different to 'before' it is definitely a 'good different'. We have so much fun doing this together.

Don't get me wrong, as much as our tiny is now a foodie who is able to get through a 'restaurant' dinner this in no way means that I don't take absolute joy and pleasure when we can go for a meal as a two! When we can talk to each other about something other than 'coco melon', have a glass of wine, take our time and enjoy our food whilst it is still hot. Enjoy a meal without having to do a mid-dinner nappy change, colour some very entertaining children's menu and bribe her with a treat to just get her through the gap between dinner ending and desert coming. I have not been consumed and fooled by this tiny human to have forgotten just how enjoyable a meal for two is!

My Husband

Who became a stranger for a short while amongst the whirlwind of chaos that erupted in our lives but who I never stopped loving.

I have written and deleted this chapter so many times, it is the hardest part for me to write so I will keep it brief.

To my husband who I love completely. Who I pushed away for far too long. We were lost for a while but as my own inserted line from our favourite film goes, "You're not lost anymore, I found you."

The pre-baby couple that exists is strong, spends all of their free time together doing the things they love. Holidays, that involve two weeks lying on their backs baking peacefully to a lovely shade of brown only moving to the bar for a cold drink and the restaurant for a delicious meal. Mooching around town stopping for coffee, lunch and dinner on the weekend. Going to the gym and maybe a steam room and a swim afterwards. Having a lazy day just because you can and because you can't be arsed to do anything else on this cold, wet day.

That was our normal for ten years before our tiny human arrived. So you can imagine the absolute shock to both of our systems when our beautiful girl made her appearance and the peaceful, selfish lives we had become so used to living, enjoyed living, became absolute chaos!

We knew things would change, of course we did. We wrongly and very naively assumed that we could continue to live the life we had been living and our tiny would just slot in to the rhythm and routine of things.

In that first week we realised that everything was going to change, everything had changed and we were not quite sure we liked it. This upheaval to our lives was something we were not even close to being prepared for. We hated it.

Hormones rife and a whole lot of sleep deprivation only meant that there was a dramatic shift in our relationship. I immediately felt wholly responsible for the fact that we were not enjoying this. By feeling this way I had overwhelming paranoia that the end of our relationship was looming.

In those two minutes you have to glance in the mirror at yourself after a shower you see a stranger looking back at you. You wonder if your body will ever heal, if the bleeding will ever stop, if the fear that is written all over your face and consuming your entire being will ever go. I didn't like myself but deeper than that I didn't know myself. So to him, who was I?

I felt so distanced from my husband, I wanted him to tell me we would be okay. He didn't. He couldn't. If I was finding this hard he was finding this close to impossible. We didn't talk about it. We uttered a few comments about it to one another. I don't know about him but I was so scared to really talk to him about it because in my hormonal, fear-stricken state I knew I probably wouldn't like what we would have both said or how the conversation would have ended.

Instead of talking we distanced ourselves from one another. We were there together but sharing no truth of how we were really feeling. I think we both knew how we were feeling deep down but in not talking there was a distance between us that to me, seemed huge. I was frightened of it, we had always been so close, so tight, so honest with one another.

I am not sure when things changed and they didn't change overnight but I decided I think somewhere around the twelve week mark that I had to get a grip of this situation. Wallowing in self-pity was not going to change this. So I faked it. I pretended I was good at this whole motherhood thing. I was excessive. I made it my business every day to make sure my tiny was clean, fed, happy and entertained all day every day. I made sure my house was clean. I made sure the washing was done. I cooked meals for when my husband got home from work. It meant I didn't stop, I quite literally didn't stop but for me it is what got me through and tipped me from the point of looming darkness to "having" this. In my own mind if those around me but particularly my husband thought I had this then everything would quickly alter back to how it was before. Most importantly for me though, my relationship would go back to how it was before.

It took time. It took a lot of work, a lot of compromise and a whole lot of adjustment from both of us. We got there though. I think we probably came out better for it. We did have an honest conversation eventually, though when she was far passed the baby stage and well in to her toddler stage. By which point we were good. I wish that conversation would have happened earlier maybe it would have closed the distance sooner, although on reflection maybe it would have made it worse. I think perhaps we were both (I definitely was) too fragile to be that honest too soon.

If I could do this whole thing again, this is the area I would focus on the most, our relationship, because when we finally got this whole parenting thing together we were very good at it and those difficult and challenging days became so much easier to handle. They were the things we had secret giggles about and laughed about for hours in the night when our tiny was cosied up in bed.

For our first Christmas together we had this romantic idea of going to the Christmas market with our tiny. We would walk, it wasn't far, she would love seeing all the Christmas lights and we would enjoy a mulled wine! We hate mulled wine but we had got caught up in the romance of the idea. We had got so caught up in the idea that I brought out my famous annual stew. The trip was a disaster, it was massively overwhelming for our tiny, she hated the lights, hated the people. We tried, almost begging her to enjoy it just long enough for us to have a Christmas photo together. We gave up and decided it was best to accept that the idea was a stupid one and walk home. We laughed all the way home, my husband referring to our trip as the 'prefect Kodak moment'. Three months prior to this, we would have dealt with this situation by not talking about it, being very angry and pissed and never mentioning the whole ordeal ever again but by this point we laughed all the way home about it. We still laugh about it now.

So, hold it together, talk to each other, if it's really shit talk about how really shit it is together. It helps, it really helps. The all-consuming newborn phase goes by so quickly. When you're in the midst of it you think it will be this way forever, I did!

Stay close, stay strong and be honest. You won't be lost forever.

I love you.

It Gets Good

Once you are passed the shit storm of the newborn phase, once you accept that your life has changed forever but actually you quite like this new version, once you accept that some things will be on hold for a little while, then you will start to enjoy it.

Becoming a mama is the hardest thing I have ever done. I put that ahead of a relocation disaster and running a failing business. The struggles were real, I had never felt anything like it. To be given something so precious, something so longed for and then hating every minute, feeling like you have made such a terrible mistake is awful. You hate yourself, you hate your life and you would do anything in those first days (months in my case) to rewind and make this go away. Somewhere along the way those feelings change. You start to get the hang of what you are doing. You start to get good at what you are doing and finally you start to enjoy what you are doing, being a mama!

When the enjoyment sets in and the fear subsides it gets good. It gets really good. In fact it gets so good that the days and weeks start flying by and that return to work date approaches fast.

You enjoy your little routines, you enjoy each other, you have little quirks, signs, jokes, that only the two of you get. I remember my mum telling me in those early days that when I was just a baby we were best friends. She had so much enjoyment out of me. In our early days I didn't understand this, how could you be best friends with a tiny human who doesn't speak. Now I understand. You don't need to have a verbal conversation, you somehow learn to communicate in your own way. Mother's instinct! You can spend hours playing, eating, laughing and your tiny human can't speak a word. That in itself is something so special.

Our tiny humans are so pure, so innocent, so real! When they start to develop their own personality and character you long to know what they are thinking as you push them in their pushchair and they daydream. You want to know that they are happy. You want to know that they know how much you love them.

Now this all sounds like very mushy shit, especially if you are reading this in those early days when you feel like this constant feeding, changing, winding, sterilising and napping is never ending. When you are looking at this tiny human and feeling nothing. When you are looking at yourself in the mirror and see only a stranger staring back at you. When you are feeling all of those things you don't want to read someone spinning the bullshit of how wonderful it is, because to you right now it is never going to be wonderful, this hell is never going to end and you are never going to enjoy this. You will! I was you not so long ago.

Don't get me wrong, it would be heavenly to enjoy lying in bed with my husband on a Saturday morning till eleven a.m., watching morning TV and reading a book. To sit in a beer garden when the sun is shining only moving to walk to the next beer garden. To pop to the shop at nine p.m. because you fancy some popcorn and beer. However parking all of these little things, to be the highlight of someone's day is not much of a comparison really. To your tiny human you are the whole world and very quickly they become yours.

When the fear subsided I looked forward to my beautiful

baby girl every day. She is our joy, our entertainment, our world. It hasn't been plain sailing and it hasn't been easy but now those hard days are over it is good, really good!

Now I feel lucky, now I appreciate her. I look at her gorgeous face and I feel such overwhelming love. I never thought it would come but now I never imagine feeling any other way.

It doesn't mean there aren't days that she doesn't drive me absolutely crazy. Having a child as I am still learning is never easy all of the time. The phases are constant, there are always challenges they just differ at each stage. My tiny human is the sassiest queen I have ever known, she has the ability to push every single one of my buttons at the same time. No one else has this ability. She is me! When her Beyonce self comes at me with all her drama and attitude (honestly she has attitude) I want to be mad, sometimes I am mad but within seconds I am trying to conceal my grin and laughter because that little sassy pants yelling at me is ME. Not that I am a yeller, I am the opposite but she says the things I always say in my head, she has no filter, but that just makes her even more awesome in my eyes. For now anyway!

Some Days Are Really Shit and That's Okay!

Tiny humans have off days too! Just like we have days where hormones are raging and you want to punch anyone that looks at you never mind speak to you. Your tiny will have those days too. That's okay. Those are the days you will enjoy ten minutes of absolute silence and stillness just after you have kissed your tiny goodnight and cosied them down to sleep.

There is a pressure put upon us to feel that every day of being a mama should be enjoyable. Maybe it is self-pressure, or the pressure of those around us but there is most definitely a pressure. In reality to enjoy every single moment of every single day simply cannot be the case. Why would it be? Why should it be?

We all have those days where you wake up and you just feel a bit shit. I'm not talking about now, I definitely had those days before baby, before the responsibility of keeping my precious tiny human alive. There is often no explanation for the sudden dip in mood, you just know that today is going to be a shitty day and that is okay. We can't always be on our best form. It would be abnormal to sail through life in the same temperament all of the time. With all of those hormones flying around the place there has to be a change in mood, in my opinion. We naturally go up and down and if we can balance off somewhere in the middle for the majority of our days then that is a success. For some, these shit days may only come once a year for others they can be once a month, once a week, whatever the case generally a shitty day is something we drag ourselves through wishing bed time will arrive as soon as possible so that we can wake up to a new day. A better day, an enjoyable day!

The reason I am harbouring this point of those shitty days is because our tiny human is allowed to have these days too. When your tiny human has been around for about nine months, you have enjoyed, yes I actually said it, *enjoyed* many days with them. You have shared so many special moments together. You can interact with them so much more at this point, you can giggle with them, play with them, lovingly watch them for hours at a time and you enjoy one another's company. For the most part anyway! Then there will come a day where nothing you do for them is good enough. You think, shit I've lost it, I don't know what I am doing. These days are so few and far between now that it knocks you sideways. They don't want to be held, they don't want to be put down, they don't want to play, they don't want to go in the pushchair, they don't want to go in the car seat. While these days are tough it is okay mama, let them be grumpy, allow them to have a day where they are just out of sorts. Hold them tightly when you can, when they have a meltdown for absolutely no reason give them a cuddle, distract them with anything and everything around you, stick to your plans, stick to your routines. Just get through the day because tomorrow is not far away and these days are passing by so quickly now.

When I am having a shitty day I don't really want to talk, I don't want to do any more than I have to do, sometimes I don't have much of an appetite. Your tiny human is likely feeling just like you do on your shitty day. It doesn't make them days any easier because a grumpy baby for a day makes for a very long day. You will most definitely clock watch hopeful that bed time is approaching soon. Again this does not make you a bad mama, tiny human is not the best of company on these days. I wouldn't want to be around me on a shit day so the same rules apply. No special treatment here tiny human! These days can feel so long, you can feel like you have a newborn all over again.

To feel a pressure to make every day the best day is not realistic. You are only setting yourself up for a fall if you do this. Many of us have a shit day in work but at five p.m. we can sign out, think fuck it, go home, eat food, shoot the shit to relieve the pressures of our day, and maybe have a glass of wine to take the edge off. We are so glad the day is over but we don't carry guilt that we have had a shit day in work. Maybe we should approach a shit day as a mama in the same way. We can't be perfect all of the time, because that is just not real life. We would be lying if we said we enjoyed every second of every day as a mama. It is hard, it is exhausting and a day of a grumpy baby is wearing. All we can do, all we can ever do for our tiny human is our best!

I have always tried my best at everything I do in life and in turn have always been very self-critical however as a mama this self-critical element is through the roof. On a bad day I will doubt myself, question myself and often send myself quite quickly into a panic just like I did when she was a newborn. I find that I lose all rationale on these days. If I have for one moment in a day thought to myself 'I can't wait for bed time' or worse still, 'stop crying, what the hell is wrong with you' I can guarantee you that night when she goes to bed I will beat myself up for hours. I will feel like the most awful human in the world. When really I should just accept the fact that she was a bit annoying today. There is nothing wrong with that, it's true!

We want to be the best mama in the world, we know this the instant we find out we are pregnant. We want our tiny human to be happy all of the time. We want to take them here, there and everywhere. We want to be their best teacher, their best cook, their best friend, we just want to be the best we can and give them the best life. It is great that this is what we strive to be to our most precious gift in life but in reality we can only do our best and mama to that tiny human, to whom we are their whole world our best is good enough. Even on our best form they can still be grumpy and that is okay.

The worst days for me are those when she "hates" me and "loves" everyone else. When I mentioned before that she has no filter she makes no exception for me. It stings, and even though I tell myself she doesn't mean it, she doesn't know what she is doing, it still bloody hurts. I can't help but take it personally. I wish I could enjoy the break, the fact that she wants to be climbing all over her daddy or nanny instead of me but I don't. I start to think about what I could have possibly done to piss her off so much. Then I realise I haven't done anything. Other than be her mum. She must feel so completely and utterly loved by me that she knows she can treat me like a piece of shit for a day and my love wont falter in any way whatsoever. She's right, don't get me wrong but still, it's harsh.

It is in those moments when she is being an absolute monster to me that I think of my mum. I think of all the times I was short with her, lost my temper, the years of being a completely unreasonable teenager demanding to have a 'camping' night in the woods with my friends and being totally and utterly pissed off and fuming that my mum said no. The real appreciation of this relationship wasn't fully there until I became a mum. Yes I appreciated my mum as much as I thought possible but now I see it from her eyes. The level of appreciation I have now comes from a different place.

Return to Work

Returning to a part of your "normal" pre-baby life. Taking back a little bit of you! You thought you would be excited, but it's scary. You will drink nice hot coffee though and be able to have a solo pee.

And just like that the year is over! After those first few months that seemed to drag, when you thought that those sleepless, panicked, lonely nights would last for an eternity you look back and realise just how fast that year has gone. Now that your return to work is looming you don't want this to be over. The emotions are high. How is this going to work? My tiny human needs me, full time, how is she going to manage without me? Or is the truth that I need her? How am I going to manage without her?

I had done two keeping in touch days when my tiny human was twelve weeks old. I had begged my boss for these days because it seemed so much more appealing to go to work rather than to stay home in my living nightmare. Those two days helped me immensely. I felt sick for the entire time, I missed my tiny human, I worried about her, and I yearned to get home from the office to be with her. They helped me to feel the things I hadn't yet felt. Towards the end of my maternity leave I did a couple more keeping in touch days. I didn't want to do them, it was only emphasising the point that I was going back to work and I didn't want to go back at all, let alone for these days.

I love my job, I love the team I work in. I am so lucky to

have this I know because so many people hate their job. Even so this did not make it any easier. I reduced my hours to return to work part time, again so lucky I was in a position to be able to do this. We had spent every day of the last year together. My tiny human had become my sole purpose. I knew that it would be fine, that the thought was more frightening than the reality. It would be an adjustment for both of us and not necessarily a bad one. It would be a positive thing for her to spend time with grandparents and time without me. It would be a positive thing for me to have a life outside of her. It would be a positive thing for our family, for her to see that mama and dada go out to work.

In the month before my return to work I did what would be my final keeping in touch day, before my actual return date. It was to attend an awards event, a celebration, a nice thing to attend. I arrived at the venue and as I got just outside the doors to walk in, I freaked. The anxiety hit me like a punch in the face, I was shitting myself. Why? I don't know why, I had never felt that way about anything work related before but the last thing I wanted to do was walk in the room. I was petrified. One of my friends came to me, what's wrong she said, you look scared. I was. I walked in with her and did everything I could to avoid eye contact with everyone and anyone that might possibly want to talk to me. As people approached me I panicked, I had nothing to say to them. Other than talking about my tiny human I had nothing to say. I didn't want to have become one of those people that had nothing to talk about other than their baby. I couldn't wait to get out of there.

After the event I got home and I felt low. In truth I had been feeling flat for about two weeks before this but with no explanation. Although my return to work was looming it felt so much more than that. While I was majorly sad to be going back to work and the thought of not spending every day with my tiny human pained me to the stomach I wasn't anxious about it. I knew that she would have the best time with her grandparents, she would be spoilt rotten with love and attention for those three days I was in work. This is not what was causing my anxiety.

On the Monday morning of the following week we woke up and came downstairs, I was stood in the kitchen preparing our breakfast. I peered through to the living room where my tiny human was sat on the floor amongst her many toys and she started dancing. That was me finished, I sobbed in the kitchen. What was it? What was making me like this? These high emotions and anxiety had been a constant for just over two weeks now and I couldn't pinpoint what it was. I took a moment to reflect.

What I realised in that moment of watching my tiny human living her best life dancing in the living room whilst I sobbed in the kitchen was that she had made me. She was my confidence, she was my side kick, she was my best friend. Without her, who was I? This to me was weird, given my rocky start to motherhood. It had taken me what felt like far too long to learn how to be a mama, but I had become quite good at it. In this transition and learning I had lost the person that I was, the person I was before I had my beautiful baby. I had found myself not knowing what clothes I liked, what interests I had, how to hold a conversation. When I was with her I could walk into a room of strangers with confidence, I could start conversations with ease and I knew who I was. Without her I was lost!

Once I had realised that this was the issue I spoke to my husband. I didn't want to because I didn't want him to think, oh for fuck sake my wife has gone bat shit again. He was wonderful though, he said he totally understood and that surely it must be normal for mamas to feel this way. After spending the last year of your life putting them at the forefront of everything you do, you are now taking just a little bit back to be you once again. After talking it through my anxiety went away, I could deal with it now and begin to reinvent myself. The pre-baby me had mostly gone so now I was beginning my next transition of returning to work and finding myself. I realise this sounds like a load of hippy shit but honestly I thought the intense emotions, the anxiety and days of crazy bitch were long behind me but here she was once again for hopefully the final time.

My first day back to work was here. I got ready for work, woke my tiny human and got her ready for her day. Today my tiny human was to spend the day with my dad and step mum. I cried all the way to drop her off, I sorted myself out for the swap over and then I cried the whole hour it took me to drive to work. I was angry! So angry, why do we have babies just to hand them over to someone else. None of this made sense to me. I sat in my car outside the office, I sorted my face out, painted my best smile on and began my day.

My work colleagues were wonderful they had made a big fuss of welcoming me back. My dad and step mum did a wonderful job of sending me lots of photos to keep me updated on her day (really to let me know that she was completely fine and having the time of her life). I finished work at four forty-five and couldn't get to her quick enough to pick her up. I was so happy to see her and she was to see me! Day one over, success.

Now the sleeping nightmare began. I've read a lot about separation anxiety, it's a good thing, a milestone apparently. However, it is not such a good thing when you are back in work and have to be up at five-thirty a.m. and your tiny human is struggling to sleep. These sleepless nights lasted for six months! The first six months I was back in work, I felt as though I had no sleep. In fact I didn't just feel that way, I actually had no sleep. Somehow, like in those newborn days you just manage. Lots of coffee and on autopilot you manage.

What I learnt immediately was that I had to be organised. I had to quickly establish a new routine and be super organised. Monday became cleaning and shopping day, Tuesday was play day and the rest of the week was work . The mornings were quick, I had to get myself ready, wake my tiny human (who would usually fall asleep just in time for me to get ready for work) and get her to whichever grandparent was having her for the day. In the evening it was, pick up, dinner, bath, bottle, bed and then packing her things ready for the next day and getting my things ready for work. We soon got the hang of it. Essentially you know that limited 'me' time you have on maternity leave, well that becomes pretty much non-existent. 'Me' time does not exist, unless you count work of course.

By week three the anxiety was completely gone. My legend of a tiny human had quickly settled into her new routine. She was loving her days that I would work, she was completely ruined and to be truthful I think she appreciated me more on our days together. I was probably pretty boring seven days a week so I think she was pleased for a bit of variety. It also made it easier for me to have a night out with my husband on those lovely occasions you manage to steal a whole evening for just the two of you, you appreciate those moments so much more than you did pre baby too! In a lot of ways work did us good, our family good, me good and my relationship good.

I still have a love, hate relationship with the whole working mama thing if I am truthful. I know I am so lucky to be able to work part time and have a balance. I do like the motherhood escape, especially if my tiny human is running a monster week instead of a monster day but I do hate the rushing. I always feel there is a pressure, a time pressure. There are only so many hours in a day, to clean, cook, bathe, organise, work and everything else that goes with being a working mama I feel a pressure on our time. It is not as easy just to 'let things slide' because it will always catch up on you. I am very lucky though, I work out of choice and I am extremely lucky to have that choice. Personally, to mother like you don't have a job and to work like you don't have a child is just not possible. Not for me anyway.

Not every day is perfect, some days I suck at my job and some days I suck at being a mama but I will always try my best, and that will just have to be good enough.

What I have learnt in all of this is, is to try and be a perfectionist in motherhood is an absolute certainty to buying a one way ticket to headfuck island. Life is not perfect, but the most perfect moments so far in my motherhood journey have been those moments when my day is utter chaos. The days I have decided I am just not going to get dressed because I am fucking exhausted and my tiny does not want to sit in the bathroom while I have a shower.

Those days when my house looks like 'Toys 'R' Us' has been ransacked, the breakfast dishes are still laying on the table at three p.m. and my tiny has decided that the best game ever is to wrap me in a rug and jump all over me. Those days when I just let everything go, let my hair down and give myself to her completely are the days I laugh the most, the days I tuck her up in bed and feel like I am winning at life.

My Mama

Who I look at with a whole new level of love and appreciation since becoming a mama myself!

My mama was there a lot in my babies first year, when my husband went away for work, she would move in to help. My mum, I have mentioned her before, she is the woman who fears nothing. She is also brutally honest, holds a strong opinion and loves a debate. So, I took the risk and asked her what she thought of me in those first weeks and months of becoming a mama…

1. *How did you see me in those first weeks?*

I saw you as someone who was trying there hardest to look like they weren't overwhelmed.

2. *Did your perception change? If so, when?*

Yes, quite quickly, I would say within a month. You were making decisions. I can't remember what time or what day, but I was going to do something for the baby and you said no don't do that and you instructed me on what to do. It was the first time you were confident that your decision was right. Previous to that you were always looking for a second opinion. Although it was only small things it was enough to say you were getting on with it, you were taking control.

3. *Did you have concerns or worries?*

Massive concerns in the first month. I genuinely thought I would have to give up my job to do this with you. My one massive concern wasn't the basics but that if you didn't bond with her nobody could make you. This was difficult for me because I didn't understand it. Outwardly you looked okay, the baby was dressed and looked well, the house was clean, you had a routine. I couldn't understand your struggle, it was alien to me. You're as soft as shift and very dependable for anybody, you're always there for everybody so if you weren't bonding with the baby there was a major problem because you are completely selfless, thoughtful and caring.

4. *From what you saw, how was I coping?*

Logistically fine, emotionally you were struggling.

5. *From what you saw, was I enjoying?*

No, I don't think you did enjoy the first few weeks. I think the fear was totally overwhelming you.

6. *Could you relate?*

I could relate to the sense of responsibility that hits you when you have a baby.

7. *How do you see me now as a mother?*

I think you are a fantastic mother. I think it has had no bearing on the baby whatsoever. I think it is really important to know that. I look at you now and you have produced this happy, healthy beautiful baby.

8. *As my mama, how was the experience of watching your baby become a mama and struggle?*

At first, I thought you had had a complete personality change. A new baby in a family is a massive adjustment to the whole family even the extended family. When that baby is born you try to contribute in whatever small way you can. For me all of a sudden, I was not recognising my daughter and it was frightening, frightening for all of the people close to you. I think I just didn't recognise you because you are so caring as a person. I could feel that you were not enjoying this tiny little bundle. For me, my life had stayed the same I was only going to have the benefits and happiness of this little baby, it was all wonderful and rosy to me but the person who was tending to that baby all night long, my daughter, was struggling like hell. It started to manifest, and I didn't recognise you.

I never did the nursing and caring you did that, I just did housework and helped around the house. You made the decisions as a mother. We had discussions but you made the decisions. It was only for about a month as I remember it. You've never suffered with mental health before, you presented that everything was okay. If you hadn't had cried that day, I never would have known anything was wrong.

A mother's love and worry does not change or falter no matter how old you are. Being honest with my mum in the worst of days was not easy but it gave me someone to talk to. It allowed me to acknowledge and accept how I was feeling.

Becoming a mother, myself has given me a whole new appreciation of my mother. I look at her and I don't think I can come close to the mother that she is. For my whole life, even now, she has always put me first. I have always felt as though I have been and still am her priority (my siblings too). If I need something, anything, no matter what time of day, she is there. Sometimes she is even there when I don't ask her to be. Interfering mother she would say but I think she just knows that I need her even before I realise it.

I don't know if I give as much of myself to my daughter as she gives of herself to me. I would like to think I do but honestly, I am not sure. I am not sure I could ever give myself completely to anyone, not without feeling the restraint of it. She is completely selfless when it comes to her children. It is admirable, though I think she is definitely deserving of taking a bit of herself back now.

In the moments my tiny human has become a monster and wants anyone but me, and this does include complete strangers, despite telling myself she doesn't mean it, she doesn't understand it, it still hurts. In these moments I wonder how many times I hurt my mother. Especially as I got older, when you do understand the words you are using, when you are completely unreasonable and irrational. How many times did I catch her right in the juggler that she had to steal herself to the bathroom to catch the tears in secret. In secret so that she didn't upset me by letting me know that I had really upset her. I am sorry mum, I didn't know you had feelings too. I didn't know that regardless of what I said or did your love would not falter. You would take in my words, make excuses for me and carry on loving me endlessly without uttering a word of your hurt to me.

I can't compare our mothering, we are different in the many ways that we are similar but I do know that as a child and as an adult I have always felt loved. I have always felt the priority. I have always felt like I am her whole world. I have never doubted that, ever. I know that she would be there for me always and I cannot and do not want to imagine a life without her.

For my mum who I love endlessly, who I appreciate more than ever and who I cannot thank enough for her unfaltering, everlasting love. There is no one quite like you. I will try, but I already know that I won't even come close to mothering like you do. You raised an impossible bar to reach.

I love you always.

The End

That was our first year. The highs, the lows, warts and all. I did warn you I would be honest. Hopefully honest enough to make you feel that you are not alone but not too honest that you think I am a monster. Actually, if you do think I am a monster then well done you for getting through your first year, but particularly the newborn phase without feeling any of my truths. Also, sorry that you wasted your money on buying my book, you probably didn't need this one! I did try to give you a clue in the name of the book because in those first weeks and months for me it really was a welcome to MOTHERFUCKINGHOOD.

For those of you that got me though, that felt my pain, my anxiety, my truth, I hope that you enjoyed it or at least got something from it. When I was in my darkest of days I needed this book, I searched for it, but I couldn't find it. There were lots of blogs out there and they were helpful, but I needed more. I needed to hear my truths were normal. I needed to not feel alone in this scary motherhood world. I needed someone to tell me, very specifically, that they had felt like I had felt and had survived it.

I wanted to write this and put it out there for anyone after me who is sweating their way through their first days as a new mama and quite frankly hating it. For those who are wondering why the fuck they decided it would be a good idea to bring this newborn chaos into their lives.

You can see my struggle was real and for me that made this book so important. It has been tough to write and even tougher to read. I know that for many people they will find this book possibly awful but for those who need it, I truly hope that this gives you some hope, some light at the end of what feels like a never ending dark and gloomy tunnel.

What I didn't know at the beginning of my story was that everything I was feeling was normal. That it wasn't just me who felt like they had taken on a colossal challenge and then decided much too late that they didn't want to take part anymore. If I had known in those first days that this was normal but more so that it would pass so quickly, I honestly believe I would have been okay. I am not saying it would have been easy, it is never going to be easy. Hormones and sleep deprivation alone are enough to make anything difficult, but I would have felt a lot more secure in my mind. I spent most of those first days thinking I was absolutely losing my mind and that petrified me.

And so, as I end this book, I share with you that maybe, just maybe, there is consideration to do this all over again!

So, if it was really that awful why on earth would we choose to do it again. The short-lived pain is overtaken by so much love, fun and enjoyment that it is worth doing ten times over. Though for the sake of my grey hairs and eye bags I will hopefully do it just once more. Don't panic, I haven't become one of those mamas, a few years on who has forgotten just how bad that newborn phase was for me. I am going into this with my eyes wide open, I have much more of a realistic expectation this time round. I know those first days, weeks and months will be hard but this time I would spend much more time without my make up on, in my pyjamas, soaking it all up. It is bittersweet, I wish that the approach I take, if we are lucky enough to have one more is the approach I took the first time round, but I cannot change that. What we have now is perfect and so I wouldn't change my story for the world. To get what we have now may not have come at all if we changed our story. Who knows maybe I will find it just as hard, I don't think so, but I am willing to take the risk because it is more than worth it once you are through the storm.

I wish you lots of luck and send you lots of love. Remember to talk, be honest and drain every bit of support you have around you. Don't be too proud or afraid to ask for help, take that pressure off yourself and give no shits about anyone. Focus on you and your family when you are battling your way through your first weeks, everything else can and will wait.

With lots of love and a whole lot of newborn cuddles,

J.D.